Public Participation
in Public Decisions

John Clayton Thomas

Public Participation in Public Decisions

New Skills and Strategies for Public Managers

Jossey-Bass Publishers · San Francisco

Substantial discounts on bulk quantities of Jossey-Bass books are
available to corporations, professional associations, and other
organizations. For details and discount information, contact the special
sales department at Jossey-Bass Inc., Publishers. (415) 433-1740; Fax
(800) 605-2665.

For sales outside the United States, please contact your local Paramount
Publishing International Office.

TCF Manufactured in the United States of America on Lyons Falls
Pathfinder Tradebook. This paper is acid-free and 100 percent
totally chlorine-free.

Credits are on p. 211.

Library of Congress Cataloging-in-Publication Data

Thomas, John Clayton.
  Public participation in public decisions : new skills and
strategies for public managers / John Clayton Thomas. — 1st ed.
      p.   cm. — (Jossey-Bass public administration series)
  Includes bibliographical references (p.   ) and index.
  ISBN 0-7879-0129-6 (alk. paper)
  1. Public administration—Decision making—Citizen participation.
2. Political participation. I. Title. II. Series.
JF1525.D4T56 1995
350.007'25—dc20   95-13425
                                                              CIP

FIRST EDITION
HB Printing   10 9 8 7 6 5 4 3 2 1

The Jossey-Bass

Public Administration Series

Contents

To my sons, Jason and Bryan

Preface

During the last third of the twentieth century, the American public has become increasingly involved in managing public organizations. Since the mid 1960s, a convergence of new legislative requirements, growing citizen activism, and changing professional values has legitimated citizen roles in programmatic areas as diverse as community development, crime prevention, mass transportation, environmental planning, and hazardous waste disposal (see Advisory Commission on Intergovernmental Relations, 1979).

"The new public involvement" has transformed the work of public managers. Many of those who once worked behind the scenes and out of the public eye now work closely with citizens and citizen groups on an everyday basis to administer the public's business. For these managers, public participation in the managerial process has become a fact of life. In the future, this may become the case for even more managers, since the public's demand for involvement does not seem to be abating.

The new public involvement forces public officials to answer difficult questions. Which issues would benefit from public participation and which would not? If public involvement appears desirable, what form should that involvement take and who should be involved? And perhaps above all else, by what means should these determinations be made as issues arise?

The stakes in answering these questions are high. Public participation that is not well planned can pose serious threats both to public management and to American democracy. As Cupps (1977, p. 478) has warned:

In spite of the proven accomplishments of citizen groups in some policy areas, there is a growing body of data to support the contention that public participation which is automatic, unrestrained, or ill-considered can be dangerously dysfunctional to political and administrative systems. . . . To the extent that we permit non-governmental groups, publicly oriented or private, to have a decisive voice in determining public policy, we add to the crisis of legitimacy and authority affecting all of our political institutions.

These concerns carry all the more weight in an era in which public managers, faced with fiscal austerity and low public confidence in government, are also being told to increase effectiveness and efficiency. Although public involvement conceivably can help in that effort—by improving the fit of public programs to citizen needs, by increasing community acceptance of programs, or by stimulating citizen assistance in the operation of programs (see Yin and Yates, 1974; Whitaker, 1980; Levine, 1984)—it can also threaten both effectiveness and efficiency. Public participation in scientific issues, for example, has been said to "lead to administrative delays, excessive constraint based on short-sighted goals, and, ultimately, to dangerous social control over scientific inquiry" (Nelkin, 1984, p. 29).

In the end, public managers are left with a difficult and complicated task. They are expected to involve the public more in the affairs of government, but they are not told exactly when and how to do so; they are told only that the involvement must be accomplished without cost to either the effectiveness or efficiency of government.

This book was written to assist in resolving this dilemma. Its purpose is threefold: first, at the level of theory, to clarify how public participation fits into managerial theory; second, for practitioners, to provide "how to" guidelines for public managers who must decide when and how to involve the public; and third, to satisfy my own normative democratic goals, to increase the level and the effectiveness of public participation in public management and decision making.

The third purpose warrants more comment. It is my belief that the public has not been sufficiently involved in the making and implementing of decisions that will affect it. My belief derives in part from the democratic values to which I subscribe. In Benjamin Barber's language, our democracy is too "thin" (1984, p. 151); we need a stronger democracy if public activities are to reflect the values of the citizenry. My belief also derives, however, from empirical research. As this book documents, more often than seeing problems from too much public involvement, I have seen how the wrong public decisions were made or how the right public decisions failed as a consequence of too little public involvement.

Increasing public participation will be achieved, I believe, if this book's first two purposes are achieved; that is, public participation will increase once public managers see more clearly how that participation fits into the managerial process and once they better understand how to pursue that participation routinely. Public managers who are more confident about when and how to invite, or *not* to invite, public participation will in fact invite more participation.

Scope and Features

This book has as its scope the place of public participation in public decisions, from large mass publics through smaller advisory committees to individuals contacting governmental agencies, and from participation in making major decisions to participation in everyday service delivery. This scope is bounded by the twin concerns for how public involvement fits into managerial theory and how, in practice, to involve the public in everyday public management. This book is thus about both theory and practice.

The book is concerned with both normative values and empirical observation. To say that public participation is essential to the success of a democracy—the normative value—is not to say that public participation should be pursued at all times or for all decisions. Empirical observation is important in learning when and how to pursue such involvement.

It is by linking theory and practice, values and observation, that this book seeks to make its unique contribution. I propose a contingency model—which I call the Effective Decision Model of Public Involvement—that applies the theoretical principles behind public involvement to the everyday questions of when and how to involve the public. The model is designed for use by public managers in assessing the value of public participation in specific issues. It is borrowed and adapted from the literature on small-group decision making (Vroom and Yetton, 1973; Vroom and Jago, 1988).

The Effective Decision Model of Public Involvement, like this book, takes as its premise that public involvement is not good or bad per se. It can be good for both the promotion of democratic values and the creation of practical advantages, but public involvement is not necessary to achieve these effects for all issues. A little or no public involvement may be best for addressing some issues; other issues may be best served by a great deal of such involvement. The trick is to be able to tell the one from the other, and the Effective Decision Model can assist in those discriminations.

The model has been tested against actual experiences with public involvement and it has been refined to reflect the lessons of those experiences. The results of the testing—the data from forty-two cases of decisions made with varying degrees of public participation—are reported and analyzed in the book, but the book is not principally a research report. The research results take a backseat to the effort to explain the relevance of the model to the practice of public management. The results do, however, constitute one of the book's special features. In addition to quantitative data, they also provide illustrative vignettes—presented in abbreviated form at various points in the book—of the application of a variety of general principles about public involvement, uses and misuses of specific forms of participation, and the roles public managers can play in producing effective public involvement.

The book also draws extensively on observations I made of public participation in municipal decision making in Cincinnati, Ohio. Most accounts of public participation report the perspectives either of public administrators/decision makers or of the actual publics, citizens, or citizen groups. In my research on Cincinnati, I sought both perspectives, and the comparisons of the two furnished many useful insights.

Audience

Public Participation in Public Decisions is written for a variety of audiences, including practicing public managers, students who aspire to become public managers, elected officials, managers in the nonprofit and private sectors, civic leaders and leaders of citizen groups, and scholars of public management. There is something here for each of these groups.

Current and aspiring public managers may benefit most from reading this book. It will give them a different and more accurate view of managerial theory by suggesting where and how public involvement fits into that theory. The book also offers these managers many practical guidelines for addressing frequent on-the-job questions about public participation. Elected officials can learn from this book on both of these counts as well. Elected officials currently must frequently turn to some form of public involvement to assist in performing their work. The process of choosing among policy options, for example, is often enhanced by information the public can provide—in public meetings, through advisory committees, and the like. In addition, many decisions about policy implementation are so controversial that elected officials must be involved and must hear from the public before any decision can be made. Knowledge about possible approaches to public participation therefore can be as essential to elected officials as to appointive public managers.

Nonprofit and private-sector managers and civic leaders may also find much of value in this book. The need to involve various publics in decision making is hardly limited to government.

Consider, for example, the many commercial and nonprofit siting questions that commonly arouse public opposition, such as proposals for a new shopping area or a halfway house for recovering substance abusers adjacent to or in a quiet residential neighborhood. Either project can quickly lead to a private developer or a nonprofit chief executive regretting his or her ignorance about how to work with the public.

The book may also be valuable to leaders of citizen groups. Those who would or could be involved as citizen representatives can learn from the advice offered to those who invite and manage that involvement. Citizen leaders would be wise, in fact, to employ the book's recommendations in working with government. After all, the recommendations are offered to make this involvement more effective for both managers *and* citizens.

Finally, I hope the book will contribute to the theory of public management and thus be of interest to scholars. The literature of public involvement has developed with a focus mostly on technique and practice, with little attention to how this new dimension of management fits into broader managerial theories. This book is intended to correct for that oversight.

Overview of the Contents

Chapter One introduces the new public involvement. It begins by making the case for increasing public involvement over what it has been in the past. The second part of the chapter explains the many choices this new involvement forces on contemporary public administrators.

Chapter Two presents a survey of the changing place of public involvement in theories of public management. It traces the evolution from traditional theories that recommended no place for public involvement, to the "new public administration" of the 1960s, which recommended a large role for the public, to a contemporary resistance that sees that involvement as often problematic. A brief history of public involvement is also presented to explain the parallel changes in how the public has been involved in the managerial process. The chapter concludes with a synthesis of the theories that recommends a substantial but circumscribed role for the public in public management.

Chapters Three, Four, and Five offer the Effective Decision Model of Public Involvement as a means for public managers to determine when and how to involve the public. Chapter Three explains the first part of the model and illustrates its use in making initial determinations about whether to involve the public in making specific decisions. Chapter Four shows how to use the model and other tools in the difficult task of defining just who should be involved when public involvement appears desirable. Chapter Five discusses how to make various decisions that call for extensive public involvement.

In Chapters Six and Seven, the discussion turns from approaches to public involvement to the mechanisms of involvement. Chapter Six examines the mechanisms that are desirable when the manager wants only information from the public, while Chapter Seven considers the mechanisms that should be used when public acceptance is desired as well. In both chapters, the mechanisms are defined and discussed in terms of when they can be more or less useful, and their use is linked to the Effective Decision Model.

Chapter Eight examines what managers can do to build a good working relationship with the public, which is essential for successful public involvement (Fisher and Brown, 1988). As this relationship grows, public involvement can move in some additional directions. Chapter Nine examines some of the advanced forms of public involvement this development may bring.

To pull the various chapters together, Chapter Ten offers a concluding perspective. First, a number of summary "dos and don'ts" are suggested for public managers to keep in mind when contemplating public participation. Second, the chapter examines how the nature of public management has changed as a consequence of public participation and a number of other forces, demanding new skills of public managers. Finally, the chapter examines the benefits that can result for democratic values from developing the skills and following the recommendations.

Acknowledgments

In one sense, this book began almost twenty years ago when I was first intrigued by the new public involvement as manifested in the unfolding relationships between neighborhood organizations and city hall in Cincinnati, Ohio. My observations of that involvement led to an earlier book, *Between Citizen and City: Neighborhood Organizations and Urban Politics in Cincinnati* (Thomas, 1986), and also began to shape the thinking that underlies the current book. I owe a considerable debt to the many Cincinnatians who contributed to my first effort and so to my current effort.

I completed much of the groundwork for this book at the University of Missouri, Kansas City (UMKC). I am grateful to UMKC, and to the Henry W. Bloch School of Business and Public Administration and the L. P. Cookingham Institute of Public Affairs, in which I worked, for their support of my work. I must give special thanks to Bill Eddy, the Bloch School dean, who encouraged me in this effort despite its occasional competition with my administrative work as director of the Cookingham Institute.

I also benefitted during my years at UMKC from a grant from the National Institute for Dispute Resolution. The grant helped to underwrite the empirical analyses reported in this book and thus facilitated my thinking more broadly about public participation as a factor in the resolution of public disputes.

I am also grateful to Georgia State University, my work home since 1993. I owe special thanks to my colleagues in the School of Public Administration and Urban Studies, who have generously assisted in the administrative work of the school, thereby allowing me time to finish this project.

The manuscript has been improved by the helpful advice of a number of readers, including Jeffrey Brudney at the University of Georgia and several anonymous reviewers. Alan Shrader at Jossey-Bass has been everything an editor should be, encouraging me to think about a book on public involvement in the first place, offering periodic helpful reminders when writing the book seemed no more than a remote possibility, and providing useful advice as the manuscript finally took shape.

Even in these days of word processing, no author completes a book without secretarial assistance. Linda Franta at UMKC helped me stay organized in preparing the original manuscript, and she was, and is, a good friend. At Georgia State, Martha Martin and Kay Brown have assisted ably at each point as the manuscript moved toward completion. I am indebted to Linda, Martha, and Kay for helping me bring this book to fruition.

Finally, I owe the greatest debt to the family I found during those years in Cincinnati. My wife Marilyn has continued to be the most helpful reader of my writing, telling me when I am making sense and, as delicately as possible, when I am not. My sons, Jason and Bryan, to whom this book is dedicated, have given me the love and camaraderie that adds a special joy to my life.

April 1995   John Clayton Thomas
Atlanta, Georgia

The Author

John Clayton Thomas is professor in and director of the School of Public Administration and Urban Studies at Georgia State University. Before coming to Atlanta in 1993, he taught for twelve years at the L. P. Cookingham Institute of Public Affairs at the University of Missouri, Kansas City, serving for six years as director of the Cookingham Institute. He has also taught at Texas Christian University and the University of Cincinnati.

Thomas has conducted research on a variety of issues in public administration and urban affairs. Underlying much of his research and writing is a concern for how citizens connect with their governments and how those connections can be improved, including an earlier book, *Between Citizen and City: Neighborhood Organizations and Urban Politics in Cincinnati*. His most recent book is *Big City Politics in Transition*, coedited with H. V. Savitch. He also has more than thirty articles in print. In addition, he has conducted applied research with governmental and nonprofit agencies, specializing in citizen and employee surveys, which he has conducted for city governments in Ohio, Missouri, and Kansas.

Thomas has held leadership posts in several national urban affairs and public administration organizations. He served from 1990 to 1992 as president of the Urban Affairs Association, and as program co-chair for the 1994 National Conference of the American Society for Public Administration. He holds a B.A. degree (1966) and an M.A. degree (1967) in journalism and mass communications from the University of Minnesota, and a Ph.D. degree (1974) in political science from Northwestern University.

Public Participation
in Public Decisions

Chapter One

The Challenge of the
New Public Involvement

The way we make governmental decisions has changed. It is no longer acceptable for such decisions to be made by a few powerful leaders who purport to act on behalf of the many but who refuse to involve the many in their deliberations. As the spread of information through education has been abetted by new technologies, more people have come to feel capable of speaking out about decisions that will affect their lives, and consequently, they have been demanding a say in those decisions. Unless the public's demands for involvement are heeded, decisions can prove meaningless in the face of the public's apathy or active opposition.

In a parallel process, the way in which scholars have viewed the role of public management has also been changing. For much of the twentieth century, public managers were seen as technicians who worked best when insulated from the public. The new view recognizes that contemporary public managers often make decisions in which public preferences are more important than technical criteria. Those public preferences cannot be known and understood by isolated public managers.

With its nature thus reconceptualized, public management has become a primary target of a new push for democratic decision making. The result is a dramatic expansion in the role of the public in public management. Contemporary public managers must know how to work with all kinds of publics, from individual citizens to small community groups to large national public interest groups. They must also be able to work with these publics in a variety of

forums, ranging from informal conversations to open public meetings to appointive community advisory committees.

The new public involvement challenges the effectiveness of
public managers. When successful, public participation can bring
substantial benefits—more effective public decisions, a satisfied and
supportive public, and most important, a stronger democracy; but
when it fails, and it has frequently failed, public participation can
leave in its wake a dissatisfied and even restive public, ineffectual
decisions, and a weakened if not faltering democracy. The risks of
failure have too often persuaded public managers to avoid or minimize public involvement. No choice could be more foolhardy. Public involvement, though neither for all matters nor always to the
same extent, is now essential for effective public management.

There are two parts to the challenge of the new public involvement. First, there is the need to understand why this involvement
has become essential. Such an understanding is a first step toward
making public participation a part of any manager's approach to his
or her work. Much of this chapter is designed to help in building
that understanding. Second, even when they have a full understanding of the necessity for public participation, public managers
may be mystified about when and how to invite that participation.
This puzzle is the subject of the latter part of the chapter.

The Roots of the New Public Involvement

The view of public involvement as integral to public management
is a relatively new idea, a late-twentieth-century innovation. Beginning in the 1960s and continuing to the present, the case for this
involvement has grown increasingly compelling.

In the 1960s, many Americans became increasingly troubled
about mistreatment of the country's African American and poor
citizens. Catalyzed by the efforts of the civil rights movement, the
persistence of racial injustice in the United States was more widely
recognized with each passing year. The perception of poverty as an
uncorrected injustice was also growing, spurred by the combination

of Michael Harrington's (1962) *The Other America* and president John Kennedy's vocal concern for America's poor.

In some circles, especially academicians and some federal policy makers, government itself was believed to be contributing to the problem by administering programs in a manner inimical to the interests of the disadvantaged. A case in point was the federal urban renewal efforts of the 1950s and early 1960s. Upon receiving federal funding to renew their core areas, most cities chose to eliminate older residential areas and replace them with new commercial developments and superhighways. In the process, large numbers of low-income residents, including disproportionate numbers of African Americans, were displaced from their homes without any offers of equivalent alternative housing. As a result, urban renewal became known colloquially as "black removal."

These stirrings led eventually to the passage of President Lyndon Johnson's Great Society legislation with its showpiece War on Poverty, a battery of federal programs targeted to combat poverty in low-income, predominantly African American areas of the United States. Concerned that these programs not fall victim in implementation to the same problems that had sapped previous urban renewal efforts of their egalitarian thrust, federal officials added legislative language requiring that programs be "developed, conducted, and administered with the maximum feasible participation of residents of the areas and members of the groups served" (Judd, 1979, pp. 302–303). With that language, the era of the new public involvement began.

The new public involvement, or citizen participation, as it was first known, differed in two principal respects from traditional public involvement. First, whereas the proper role of the public had traditionally been viewed as confined to policy making, the new public involvement focused squarely on policy implementation, on involving the public in deciding how policies, once adopted, would be put into operation. Citizens were now to be involved in managing programs. Second, in contrast to the elite bias of most traditional public involvement, such as the "blue ribbon" advisory committees

for urban renewal programs, the new public involvement broadened
the definition of relevant citizens to include those in the low-
income category. The definition was further broadened throughout
the 1970s to encompass a broad range of publics and citizen groups.
New groups were formed in those years to represent consumers,
environmentalists, and citizens concerned with other social issues,
as well as minorities and the poor (see Walker, 1983). For these
groups, the idea of citizen participation in federal programs offered
the promise of more influence over governmental programs that
affected their lives.

As a consequence, although the results of the War on Poverty
proved disappointing, with most of its component programs dis-
mantled or in disrepair in less than a decade, the idea of broadened
public involvement in policy implementation flourished, especially
in federal programs. Citizen participation requirements spread
rapidly to many federal programs between the late 1960s and mid
1970s. At the end of the 1960s only thirty-one federal grant-in-aid
programs carried citizen participation requirements; by the end of
1974, that number had more than tripled to a total of one hundred.
In another two years the number again grew, by more than half, to
encompass an additional fifty-five federal programs (Advisory Commission on Intergovernmental Relations, 1979).

As the requirements for public involvement spread, the forms
that involvement took diversified. Public involvement came to
encompass a wide range of possibilities, including the following:

• Use of citizens advisory committees to assist in Environmental
  Protection Agency efforts to implement federal water quality
  standards at the local level (Plumlee, Starling, and Kramer,
  1985)

• A series of public meetings to decide how a city will spend
  federal Community Development Block Grant funding
  (Haley, 1982)

• Mediation of a dispute over whether and where to build new public housing in a city (Gillers, 1980)

Not everyone welcomed the new public involvement, to be sure. Many state and local officials saw citizen participation as an unnecessary federal intrusion on local prerogatives. Even federal officials were troubled by the difficulties public involvement sometimes introduced to their work. Evidence from the field also suggested that, perhaps as a consequence of the frequent antipathy of administrators, requirements for public participation frequently did not result in meaningful involvement of the public (see, for example, Cole and Caputo, 1984).

A Growing Imperative

The case for public involvement has, nevertheless, grown rather than diminished. Changes in society and governance as well as normative arguments for additional desirable changes have implied that public managers as well as other leaders in and out of government face a growing imperative to involve the public in making and implementing all manner of decisions.

The root cause of this imperative is education. As people become more educated, they ask for more involvement in the decisions that will affect their lives. As Cleveland (1985, p. 192) has explained, "Knowledge is power, as Francis Bacon wrote. . . . So the wider the spread of knowledge, the more power gets diffused. For the most part individuals and corporations and governments don't have a choice about this; it is the ineluctable consequence of creating—through education—societies with millions of knowledgeable people."

The process of spreading knowledge is facilitated by the development and diffusion of new information technologies. The growth of telecommunications and the multiplication of computers has accelerated the spread of information, giving more people access to more information sooner. That broader access undermines the centralized control of information that was a principal basis for centralized decision making. In the end, as Cleveland (1985, p. 192) notes, "More and more work gets done by horizontal process—or it doesn't get done. More and more decisions are made with wider and wider consultation—or they don't 'stick.'"

As might be expected, governmental and societal institutions have lagged behind this broader process of social change. Structures designed for an age of machines and hierarchy have not adapted readily to the new age of information and shared authority. In Benjamin Barber's (1984, p. 151) terms, government has functioned as only a "thin" or minimal democracy, when what is needed is "strong democracy": "Strong democracy is defined by politics in the participatory mode; literally, it is self-government by citizens rather than representative government in the name of citizens. Active citizens govern themselves directly here, not necessarily at every level and in every instance, but frequently enough and in particular when basic policies are being decided and when significant power is being deployed."

To achieve strong democracy, decision-making procedures, especially in the public realm, must be overhauled to accommodate more extensive and effective participation of citizens. This need for overhaul is not limited to the policy formulation process. So much can happen to policies as they are put into operation that strong democracy must extend to policy implementation. The stakes in implementation can be substantial when, as is not uncommon, federal or state governments aim substantial resources at a problem, with few strictures on how the resources should be used. Even when the strictures are extensive, public administrators may still be faced with difficult decisions, with substantial consequences for society, which the policy makers either did not or could not anticipate. Excluding the public from these implementation deliberations may be tantamount to denying any democratic influence on the most important questions about a policy. It may also be a recipe for failed implementation, since spurned citizens may refuse to comply with a policy adopted without their advice or consent.

Often, citizens must do more than merely comply with implementation efforts if public policies are to achieve the desired outcomes. As Whitaker (1980, p. 240) has argued, many contemporary public services, such as education and crime prevention, that are designed to produce change in individuals can only assist the person being served to make the desired changes; whether learning new ideas or new skills, acquiring healthier habits, or changing one's outlook on family or society, only the individual served can accomplish the change. Consequently, such governmental services that lack public participation in their implementation may prove meaningless.

Strong democracy in policy implementation and administration requires that public administrators view themselves as, to borrow Terry Cooper's (1984, p. 143) terms, "professional citizens" or "citizen-administrators"—that is, as "fiduciaries who are employed by the citizenry to work on their behalf." Part of the responsibility of the citizen-administrator must be to solicit and listen to the opinions of other citizens. Only by hearing from a broad range of citizens can the citizen-administrator expect to work effectively on their behalf, bringing strong democracy to the administrative process.

A strong democracy should promote strong citizenship and a strong society. Giving people more and better opportunities to take part in their own governance can transform them from subjects of particular governmental arrangements to citizens vested in and supportive of those arrangements. Similarly, the broadening of participatory opportunities can strengthen society by assuring that the actions of government are embedded in society, rather than imposed on society.

The reasons public managers should embrace public involvement go beyond these broader democratic and societal values. Decades of experience have revealed a number of practical gains that public managers can realize from inviting public involvement, as illustrated by Case 1.1 (adapted from Thomas, 1986).

———•———

Case 1.1

Administrative Advantages in Cincinnati's Community Involvement

Public managers can gain much from public involvement, if the experience of Cincinnati is any guide. This conclusion emerged clearly from open-ended interviews in the summer of 1980 with various of the city's governmental and community leaders, including administrators from fifteen municipal departments and fourteen community council leaders.

According to the interviewees, municipal administrators in Cincinnati became extensively involved with community councils (as neighborhood organizations are known in Cincinnati) such that by the early 1980s municipal departments and the city's neighborhoods were working closely with each other on a wide range of city programs. In the process, the city's administrators discovered a number of advantages to that involvement.

1. *Better channels of communication.* Many administrators reported that the community councils proved to be useful sources of information when there were questions about community opinions. As a waste collection official commented, "At least we've got somebody as a contact in each of the communities." At the same time, the councils helped the city departments to satisfy formal requirements for community involvement. As another administrator noted, "Community councils eliminate the need for a public hearing because they hold it for you."

2. *Improved program implementation.* Several administrators argued that involving neighborhoods in departmental decisions facilitated implementation of those decisions. In the words of a housing official, "They've made it easier for programs to function

in neighborhoods because they participated in the decisions." An official in the city's engineering division reported learning about this advantage the hard way, by confronting community opposition to division-produced highways: "As we have learned from our past mistakes—or let's say, the way we operated in the past—it would be an exercise in futility to make plans for a new street or highway without involving the community. So, where we are planning a new street, we try to bring them on board as soon as possible."

3. *More services for the dollar*. Community involvement can also improve municipal productivity by enlisting neighborhoods to help in program execution and service delivery. Here neighborhoods go beyond accepting implementation to joining in the implementation. Examples of this assistance ranged from the modest, such as the highway maintenance division's use of community groups in neighborhood street inspection, to the complex, such as the cooperative effort of the recreation department and one community council in the building and staffing of a recreation center. When the Department could afford to build the center but not to staff it, the community council contracted with the city to provide the staffing.

4. *Protection from criticism*. Involving communities in decision making also reduced their criticism of municipal administrators as the community leaders who were most involved with the departments became reluctant to take conflicts beyond the departments. As one community leader said, "No one wants to go to city council with anything unless they have to." These leaders worried that their relationships with the departments could be damaged by appeals to higher authorities.

5. *Clout in the budget process*. Even as it kept complaints from going to higher authorities, Cincinnati's community involvement also increased the clout some departments had with those authorities. A number of the city's administrators argued that community councils were useful allies in the budgeting process. As one department head said, "If these people can convince city council that they

really need something, it's a good possibility that council will give it to them."

——•——

The potential gains from public involvement have achieved increasing recognition in the literature of public management and governmental reform. Public involvement figures prominently, for example, in the push for "reinventing government." Coauthors and advocates of reinventing Osborne and Gaebler (1993, p. 19) emphasize the need to "empower citizens by pushing control out of the bureaucracy, into the community." Communities, they argue, usually understand their problems better than bureaucrats do, and thus can "solve problems" where "professionals and bureaucracies [only] deliver services" (Osborne and Gaebler, 1993, pp. 66–67). The movement for managerial reform through Total Quality Management (TQM) similarly accords a prominent role to public involvement. TQM advocates argue that quality governance requires better information on customer needs, on what citizens want of government, and on how citizens feel about what they currently get from government.

The idea of public involvement now holds a prominent place in almost all contemporary theories of governance and management. At one extreme, communitarian theorists such as Barber advocate increased public involvement for building stronger communities. At the other end of the spectrum, individualistic market-based approaches view citizens as "participants" and "consumers of public goods and services," with citizen participation cast as an essential component of governmental structure (see Lan and Rosenbloom, 1992).

The Puzzle of Public Involvement

Understanding the imperative of public involvement is only the first, and perhaps the easiest, part of the challenge of public participation. Even when they accept the imperative, public managers and policy planners must still choose when, how, how often, and to what extent to involve the public. Despite frequent managerial complaints about the constraining effects of requirements for public participation, these requirements have usually been limited to directing managers to involve the public, leaving the form and extent of that involvement to the discretion of administrators. The second part of the challenge, then, of what can fairly be called the puzzle of public involvement, is, when the public is to be involved, how should that involvement be invited and engaged?

The literature of public administration contains only limited guidance for solving this puzzle. For the most part, experts on public involvement have either exhorted public managers to embrace public involvement or warned them of the dangers that lurk within. Neither perspective provides much assistance to managers who are confused over how to involve the public in resolving specific issues.

The puzzle has several parts. First, managers must decide how much influence to share with the public. In traditional public involvement, as with the "blue ribbon" advisory committees of the urban renewal era, the sharing of influence was minimal. Typically, information was shared, but influence was not. The ostensible intent of the new public involvement is to increase the influence, but by how much is often unclear. At one extreme, the public might be permitted to make decisions, with the manager serving in only an advisory capacity. At the other extreme, the public might be given a limited advisory capacity, with a possibility but no guarantee of influence, with the ultimate decision-making authority remaining with the public manager. As an intermediate option, influence in decision making might be shared by the manager and the public, although the question would remain of how much influence each would get.

Second, managers must determine who from the public to involve. Involvement could be severely limited, with the manager conferring with only a few citizens, presumably leaders of particular key groups; or entire communities might be invited to participate. The manager might also pursue both options, involving the few at one point and the many at another.

Third, managers must choose specific forms of public involvement. The options are many, including both traditional techniques, perhaps modified for contemporary realities, and newer techniques that have developed with the growth of public involvement. A short list of popular options would include the following:

1. *Key contacts.* Perhaps the simplest means for involving the public is for managers to consult with "key contacts," usually either economic leaders or leaders of other organized groups. Common historically, when managers had only limited contact with the public, this approach remains popular for informally checking community opinions.

2. *Public meetings.* When broader public involvement is necessary, public meetings are often the technique of choice, both historically and in the present. The letter of the law on many requirements for public involvement can be satisfied simply by holding a public meeting. An open meeting is scheduled, its date and time are advertised to the public, and the issue is discussed at the meeting.

3. *Advisory committees.* The advisory committee is another popular option. In this technique, representatives of various relevant groups are asked to serve on a committee which then advises on a particular policy or issue. Contemporary advisory committees often differ from their predecessors by representing a broader range of groups, including consumer groups and groups representing the disadvantaged.

4. *Citizen surveys.* Prominent among the new approaches to public involvement are citizen surveys. During the 1960s and 1970s, an increasing number of governmental agencies used questionnaire surveys to solicit citizen opinions on a wide

range of public issues and governmental services (see Webb and Hatry, 1973). If conducted on random samples of the relevant population, surveys hold the promise of providing the representative opinions that are an uncertain outcome of any other approach.

5. *Citizen contacts.* Citizens have created their own techniques of public involvement, such as increasing their contact with public agencies about various programs and issues. These contacts usually focus on very specific problems, such as a missed garbage pickup or an unfilled pothole, but the growth in their volume has added an important dimension to the public's involvement with government.

6. *Negotiation and mediation.* Some issues prove so intractable that they cannot be resolved using any of the techniques listed so far. Recognition of that fact has resulted in the growing use of negotiation and mediation, in which a third party intercedes to seek a resolution between disputants. Mediation first became popular as an approach to public involvement in the effort to resolve environmental conflicts between government, developers, and environmentalists, but the techniques have now been adapted to a broad range of issues.

To complicate matters further, seldom is the question simply a matter of which *one* technique to use. In most cases, managers must decide what combination of two or more approaches to use and at what stage to use each approach.

Finally, there are also questions about how to manage public involvement within particular forms, as well as in day-to-day contacts with the public. Finding the appropriate forms is an important step toward achieving effective public involvement, but if the appropriate form is to be used effectively, managers must also know how to interact with the public.

The stakes in solving the puzzle of public involvement are

considerable. On the one hand, assembling the pieces of the puzzle in the right pattern can bring the substantial benefits of public involvement, including more and better information for decision making, wiser decisions, and greater public acceptance of the decisions. Failure to solve the puzzle, on the other hand, can bring substantial costs, ranging from the discomfort of public acrimony to the complete paralysis of decision making.

Facing the Challenge

The nature of public decision making and the nature of public management have changed. Traditional ways of doing both have been made obsolete by the growing demands of the public to be involved in the making, implementing, and administering of public decisions. The two-part challenge of public involvement for public managers calls for, first, understanding the imperative of the new involvement, as discussed in this chapter and as explained in more detail in the next chapter, and second, solving the puzzle of public involvement by combining the various pieces into an approach that will produce an effective decision for the issue at hand. The latter part of this chapter was designed to explain the elements of the puzzle; most of the remainder of the book is intended to show how managers can successfully assemble the pieces.

Chapter Two

Finding a Practical Approach to Public Involvement

Public managers, if they have not already done so, must change how they think about their work. They must change their personal theories of public management to recognize the need for public involvement in the managerial process. This change in theoretical foundation is necessary because managers cannot be expected to engage in practices that are divorced from their beliefs about the nature of their work.

The traditional theories that public managers have been taught for interpreting their work are no longer adequate. These theories are ambivalent in their attitudes toward public participation, with outlooks varying from the hostile to the equivocal to the enthusiastic. Managers who were provided with these theories may be forgiven if their attitudes and behaviors ultimately reflect a similar ambivalence.

To work effectively with the public, public managers need a new theory, one that provides a clear understanding of the place of public involvement in the managerial process. This theory must also be capable of accommodating different stances on public involvement—hostility, equivocation, and enthusiasm—without falling victim to paralyzing ambivalence.

The purpose of this chapter is to develop such a theory. First, the principal managerial theories relevant to public involvement, which public administration education has transmitted to its practitioners, will be described. They will then be used as the basis for a proposal of a new, more practical theory, which combines the earlier theories into a balanced perspective on public involvement and suggests an additional contingent perspective, which will be elaborated in subsequent chapters.

The Traditional View: The Insulated Manager

When public administration began to develop as a distinct professional field around the beginning of the twentieth century, its first theorists took a distinctly hostile view of public involvement in the managerial process. President Woodrow Wilson (1887, p. 210), for example, warned in his classic essay of the dangers of involving the public in everyday public administration: "Directly exercised in the oversight of the daily details and in the choice of the daily means of government, public criticism is, of course, a clumsy nuisance." Wilson and other early theorists wanted to remove public administration from the pervasive political influence of the then-dominant patronage party politics. These theorists believed that public administration could not function effectively, much less build a distinct professional identity, without first being insulated as much as possible from political interference.

These beliefs took the form of an argument for a "politics-administration dichotomy." As Goodnow (1900, p. 26) explained the distinction, "Politics has to do with policies or expressions of the state will. Administration has to do with the execution of those policies." In general, these theorists viewed politics as the proper sphere for public involvement. Administration, by contrast, was viewed as an inappropriate arena for public involvement, and best left to professional administrators.

On the politics side of the dichotomy, the public's essential role in a democracy was viewed as participation in defining the "state will." That role could be exercised by individuals or by groups (such as interest groups or political parties) through voting in elections and through lobbying of elected policy makers. Those avenues of influence were viewed as the appropriate means for democratic control over public policies. As Harmon (1971, p. 174) later explained this view, "The belief that policy should be formulated exclusively by elected officials can be traced to the assumption that they are the only actors in the political system who can be held accountable by the democratic constraint of election."

The other part of the dichotomy, administration, a supposedly technical enterprise, was to be left to professional administrators. Administration supposedly did not require the value judgments that would warrant public or most other political involvement. In Wilson's (1887, p. 210) words, "Administrative questions are not political questions. Although politics set the tasks for administration, it should not be suffered to manipulate its offices." Accordingly, public administrators should be insulated and protected from politics to ensure professional rather than political administration, so that policies could then be executed with "neutral competence."

The demands of democratic accountability did necessitate a general political control of administration. Public administrators would receive their charge in the form of legislation enacted by elected representatives, and would also need to report to those representatives, who would exercise oversight of administration. This oversight function was not to be shared with the broader public. To permit public involvement here would invite the unnecessary interference of which Wilson had warned.

This was a hierarchical, top-down model of administration and democratic accountability. In the politics-administration dichotomy, once policies are formulated, influence should flow downward from elected policy makers through public administrators to the public. There was no allowance for reversing the flow to permit influence also to move up the hierarchy from the public to or through those administrators.

The politics-administration dichotomy has influenced thinking about public administration throughout the twentieth century, and for decades it was the dominant influence. During its period of dominance, such thinking inspired, for example, the council-manager form of government, in which the council was initially viewed as

responsible for formulating policy and the manager as responsible for assuring effective and efficient administration. As part of
that administrative responsibility, the manager was to supervise all
other administrators, thus insulating those administrators from
direct political influence.

The merit and civil service personnel systems that are still
prevalent at all levels of American government were inspired by
the same thinking. Under these systems, the selection of public
employees is a matter of "merit," usually measured by objective
examinations, rather than of "spoils," whereby politicians simply
hire their supporters. To protect employees from undue political
influence, termination after an initial probationary period requires
that cause be shown, that is, that clear evidence of malfeasance or
incompetence by the employee be demonstrated. With that protection, public administrators can expect to retain their jobs, regardless of how citizens or elected officials might feel about their
responsiveness.

As might be expected, this era of thought produced no major
reforms designed to encourage administrative responsiveness to the
public. Although public administrators were viewed as ultimately
accountable to the public, that accountability was to be indirect,
that is, mediated through elected officials.

The New Public Administration: Bring the Public In

Although problems with the politics-administration dichotomy
were obvious even early in the twentieth century, the dichotomy dominated public administration theory and practice until a
combination of factors prompted a rethinking in the 1960s. Some
of the influences came from outside the profession, from the policy
process itself; others came from within, from the rise of a new generation of public administration theorists.

The outside influences included federal policy changes that
asked or forced public administrators to work with the public more

closely than the politics-administration dichotomy implied was appropriate. The coming of the Great Society and "maximum feasible participation" in the mid 1960s (see Chapter One) inaugurated a new era. The new federal initiatives gave the public administration profession a practical reason to rethink its attitude toward public involvement.

At the same time, the public administration community was increasingly troubled within by allegations of bias and injustice being practiced by its members. It became increasingly common in the late 1960s for critics to characterize public administrators as the enemy of the disadvantaged, servants of the elite rather than of the "public," who were sometimes willing to pursue whatever nefarious strategy was necessary to repel the demands of the disadvantaged (see, for example, Lipsky, 1968; Kirlin, 1973). Though it was not principally the responsibility of administrators, the experience of urban renewal as "black removal" was seen as a case in point.

Stung by criticisms and spurred by changing public policies, public administration began a period of soul searching. Are these criticisms accurate, many leaders of the profession asked? If so, what can be done to correct bureaucratic injustices, as well as to reduce the seemingly growing citizen antipathy toward public administrators? And, how should the profession respond to the federal push for more public involvement? Gradually, leaders of the profession articulated a new theory of public administration, which became known as simply "the new public administration." Contained within this theory was a case for more public involvement in public management.

The shaping of the new theory began with the assertion of social equity as an important value for public administration. Todd LaPorte (1971, p. 32), one of the early contributors to the theory of the new public administration, even argued that social equity should be the profession's principal value: "The purpose of public organization is the reduction of economic, social, and psychic suffering and the enhancement of life opportunities for those inside and outside the organization." Many of the problems of public administration, LaPorte and others believed, could be traced to too little traditional concern for equity and the needs of the relatively less well-off.

The Flawed Politics-Administration Dichotomy

How could public administrators promote social equity if, as the politics-administration dichotomy implied, their work was limited to the application of neutral competence? In reality, the new theorists argued, the contemporary public administrator did more than that. In their view, the politics-administration dichotomy, whatever its historical accuracy, no longer captured the essence of public administration. The dichotomy's problems were several.

First, instead of being limited to a narrow circumscribed role in the administration of policy, as the dichotomy implied, public managers were frequently involved in policy making. Studies of policy making confirmed what many public administrators already knew, that elected policy makers routinely invited the involvement of administrators in the policy-making process by asking them for recommendations. In addition, when the line between policy and administration proved difficult to draw, public administrators often "defined 'policy' and 'administration' in a manner in which 'administration' loomed very large and 'policy' very small," thereby increasing administrative authority (Pressman, 1975, p. 36).

The increasing complexity of the governmental system also meant that many controversial policy questions could not be anticipated even by conscientious policy makers. With the development of many new federal programs in the 1960s and before, many policies that began with Congress would subsequently move through federal administration to local elective officials, sometimes mediated by state administrators, before finally reaching local administrators, to whom fell the task of actually implementing the policies in their communities. Since Congress could not anticipate all of the nuances of policy implementation, federal, state, and local administrators had to make many decisions about the shape of those policies.

Even where they did not influence policy, public administrators might still make value judgments, the theorists contended, rather than simply following unambiguous technical rules as the politics-administration dichotomy implied. Most of the new governmental initiatives of the 1960s and 1970s—efforts to organize low-income communities, to train the unemployed, to revive deteriorating cities—could not be planned according to strictly technical criteria (see Yates, 1977, pp. 80–81). Value judgments were unavoidable as the programs were put into operation.

A concurrent reconceptualization of many traditional governmental functions also reduced their previous dominance by technical criteria, forcing administrators to make value judgments there, too. Investments in public transportation, for example, had traditionally been conceptualized, according to Webber (1974, pp. 6–7), as "primarily capital investments, i.e., investments in physical plant, in physical facilities . . . ," which should be evaluated against "criteria that are internal to the transport system itself," such as "miles of highway installed, numbers of airports built, and the extent of the networks' geographic coverage." In the new way of thinking, Webber argued, those investments were viewed "as a service rather than as a facility. . . . Right off, that simple switch forces us to describe transport systems in the syntax of verbs rather than that of nouns. We must ask, What does the system do? rather than, What is it made of? How does it work? rather than, What is the geometry? . . . We are then inexorably led to the most crucial question, What should it do for whom?"

Finally, theorists also questioned the wisdom of a strictly one-way, top-down flow of influence. The evidence of administrative influence over policy making showed the empirical error in this view. There might be normative grounds, too, for believing that influence should flow from citizens to administrators as well as from administrators to elected policy makers.

If one accepts this alternative characterization of the work of public administration, it makes less sense to insulate administrators from politics and the public, as recommended in the politics-administration dichotomy. In their zeal to protect public administrators from political interference, the reformers of an earlier generation might have insulated those administrators from the publics for whom they were managing. Too many public administrators might consequently still be running programs according to technical criteria when human criteria were appropriate, thereby creating widespread bureaucratic unresponsiveness; or, as Cooper (1984, p. 147) described the problem: "What those reformers failed to foresee was the impossibility of maintaining the subordination of 'expert,' 'professional' administrators to the politicians in a modern industrial state. The power of technical expertise and specialized knowledge, the complexity of the problems to be faced, and the scale of government have tended to crowd out both the citizenry and their would-be representatives."

Nor did the fear of corruption justify excluding the public from all decision making. As Harmon (1971, p. 178) argued, "Certainly administrators are not always attuned to . . . [nor do they] act consistently with the public pulse. But surely corrupt or irresponsible behavior cannot be assumed to be the result of participative decision making . . . until so demonstrated."

The Reform Agenda

Few analysts thought that the problems of public administration could be solved by rolling back merit and civil service reforms. That could make public administration *too* political by giving elected officials and pressure groups too much power over administrators. Besides, public employees would resist such a change, and they were sufficiently powerful by the 1960s to have their way on the issue.

A better approach was to recruit different types of people in order to build a more "representative bureaucracy" (Krislov, 1974). Although by the 1960s the constituencies of governmental programs were increasingly black, female, and lower class, public administrators had remained predominantly white, male, and middle- to upper-middle-class. Perhaps, it was thought, bureaucratic responsiveness and social equity could be improved by making the bureaucrats more like their clients. Many governmental agencies accordingly undertook extensive efforts to hire employees from underrepresented minority groups.

It was also proposed that efforts be made to educate public administrators about their responsibilities to the public, to make them more aware of their ultimate accountability to the publics they served. Schools of public administration responded by giving more emphasis to these values in their curricula.

These approaches could not solve the whole problem, however. Recruiting employees from particular groups, for example, does not assure that the ideas of those groups will be adequately articulated. The employees are recruited *as employees*, after all, not as representatives. In addition, rates of employee turnover are seldom high enough for workforces to be transformed in anything less than decades, making recruitment and education long-term strategies of little help in the short term. Recruitment and education, themselves top-down approaches, also could not correct for the top-down bias of traditional management approaches. A problem of hierarchy could not be solved simply by replacing or reeducating some occupants of the hierarchy. Other means had to be found.

Public involvement offered that means. Previously neglected constituencies could be invited to join in agency deliberations, achieving more direct representation of those groups in the short term, as well as in the long term. Citizens could express their opinions on policies as they were being implemented. If public administrators were making more value judgments, public involvement would permit more citizen comment before those judgments were made. If administrators were exerting more influence over policy, public involvement would enable citizens to share in that influence. If equity were a problem, public involvement would give its victims an opportunity to gain redress.

Some theorists eventually came to view public involvement as more than only a means to enhance responsiveness. They perceived that public involvement might more broadly reflect Cooper's (1984, p. 143) characterization of the role of public administrators as "professional citizens." "The ethical obligations of the public administrator are to be derived from the obligations of citizenship in a democratic political community. These obligations include responsibility for establishing and maintaining horizontal relationships of authority with one's fellow citizens, seeking 'power with' rather than 'power over' the citizenry."

For their part, as they gained experience in involving the public, public administrators learned practical ways in which that involvement could prove useful. Whereas citizen participation was initially viewed as desirable primarily in the *planning* of programs and services, experience taught that this participation could also help in the *delivery* of services. Proponents of this perspective argued that many services could achieve the desired effectiveness only if jointly produced—or *coproduced*—by both government and citizens (see Whitaker, 1980). Evidence on police services, for example, indicated that policies could do little to prevent crime unless citizens assisted by reporting their observations of suspicious behavior. Involvement of citizens thus might enhance other elements of service effectiveness in addition to responsiveness.

Backlash: Problems in Practice

Not all reactions to the new standards of public involvement were positive. As experience accumulated during the 1970s and 1980s, a backlash of criticism developed. Growing numbers of public administrators reported one problem or another arising from their efforts to involve the public. Many practitioners and academicians were less than sanguine about the effects of the new public participation.

Coming as isolated complaints, these concerns about public involvement did not take the form of a theory. As the complaints have accumulated, however, they have built a strong case against both the new public involvement and the new public administration, which recommended that involvement. The case has at least three dimensions: the first focus is on who participates and who does not; the second, on how involvement affects the manager's job; and the third, on how the involvement affects the quality of public policy.

Imperfect Participation

Arguments for public involvement assume that increased efforts to involve citizens will result in public opinion being better represented in the administrative process, but anyone who has studied or observed participation firsthand—whether in elections, in voluntary organizations, or in other community affairs—knows that participation is often nonrepresentative. No matter what the circumstances, many who are eligible to participate do not, and those who do participate are seldom a cross section of all who were eligible. In particular, participants usually have higher socioeconomic status—better education and higher incomes—than nonparticipants (see, for example, Verba and Nie, 1972).

The new public involvement has not proved immune to these problems. Efforts to bring previously unrepresented low-income populations into the managerial process have frequently been frustrated by a lack of interest among potential participants, leading one critic (Riedel, 1972, p. 215) to argue, early in the experimentation, that "unwillingness to participate is many times more common than frustrated desire to do so." The degree of nonparticipation is graphically illustrated by voter turnout for elections of advisory boards for local antipoverty programs in the late 1960s. In cities as diverse as Philadelphia, Los Angeles, Boston, Cleveland, and Kansas City, Missouri, the proportion of eligible voters actually voting in these elections never exceeded 5 percent and sometimes was below 1 percent (Judd, 1979, pp. 307–308).

Those who do become involved through the new public involvement are frequently nonrepresentative of the larger citizen populations. Participants often represent preexisting organized groups that speak for particular special interests rather than for citizens in general. Their participation may be defensive, designed to protect the authority of existing groups from the challenge that broader public involvement might pose.

To deal with these problems, the early antipoverty programs sometimes offered money to low-income residents in exchange for their participation, sometimes for merely attending neighborhood meetings. That only invited new problems. People who participated for monetary rewards tended to pursue personal self-interest, rather than attempting to represent the interests of broader low-income populations (see Peterson, 1970). Similarly, at the organizational level, organizations that participated in order to obtain such rewards were more easily co-opted by government, losing their ability to advocate for larger populations (see Gittell, 1983).

These problems of imperfect participation are not necessarily unsolvable, but finding solutions imposes burdens on public managers. To begin with, the search for techniques to improve the representativeness of public involvement can be costly. Managers must devote considerable time to the enterprise, and may also be forced into new expenditures to hire expert outside advice. If citizens are persuaded to participate, the potential for imperfect representation forces the manager to ask, for example, do these people really speak for the citizens I need to reach? Or, if these participants appear *not* to be representative, how should their opinions be treated? Simply ignoring those opinions could engender hostility, threatening the agency's programs and the manager's credibility.

Interference with Managerial Performance

Critics argue that public involvement threatens managerial performance by making the manager's job more difficult. One threat comes from the time that public involvement demands. Time is necessary, first, to learn how to handle the process of involvement, for example, to learn how to solve the problems of imperfect representation. Next, decision making with public involvement can require more time because more people must be satisfied before a decision can be approved. Finally, if citizens are not satisfied with a decision, they may delay its implementation, adding to the time necessary at that stage. All of these demands limit the time managers have available for other parts of their jobs.

Public involvement can also be emotionally draining, because public administrators are often greeted by distrust and hostility from the citizens who become involved. As Cupps (1977, p. 482) noted, "A frequently voiced complaint is the overdramatization, hyperbole, and shrillness with which citizen groups sometimes present their case." Such dynamics can be extremely unpleasant, reducing the emotional energy the manager has for other tasks.

The unpredictability of public involvement can add to the emotional drain. As Van Meter (1975, p. 807) has commented, "The real problem for the manager comes in trying to institutionalize citizen participation so that it is permanent and ongoing . . . ," given that citizens participate "according to personal interest and available time." Rather than being stable and dependable, citizen involvement can fluctuate between intense interest and apathy; or, the citizens who participate this year may differ greatly from those who were involved last year. Coping with this volatility exacts a toll on the public manager.

Threats to Decision Quality

The most serious complaint about public involvement focuses on the distortions it can introduce to public decisions. Across a wide range of public programs, from traffic engineering to water quality to nuclear energy, well-respected professionals have warned that public involvement threatens the quality of public decisions and public policy.

The threat may take several forms. First, professionally or scientifically accepted quality standards may be challenged by citizens who do not understand the wisdom of the standards. The quality of public policy can suffer if the standards are ignored in eventual public decisions. Some scientists have argued that "science and medicine are so highly specialized that only experts are qualified to make competent judgments" (Dutton, 1984, p. 170).

Second, public involvement may lead to increases in the costs of public programs. In general, the more actors there are involved in the making of a decision, the more there are who expect a piece of the action. Adding citizen participants to the decision-making team can consequently force program costs upward. As a Cincinnati municipal official said about working with neighborhood groups, "A problem we usually find is that their involvement costs the city quite a bit of money because they want embellishments that are far beyond the reasonable utility" of the particular project (Thomas, 1986, p. 102).

Third, public involvement can deter innovation. As Cleveland (1975, p. 4) has explained, "the procedures of openness are well designed to stop things, and ill designed to get things moving. . . ." Broader consultation, whether with citizens or with other actors, increases the likelihood of someone vetoing or compromising a proposed innovation. That tendency can be beneficial if it thwarts a poorly planned change, but not if it stymies any and all change. As Cleveland (1975, p. 6) observed, "the leader who expects bold and imaginative long-range thinking to come out of a town meeting had better look for some other line of work."

Fourth, pursuing the special interests of many specific publics who accept the invitation to become involved can result in neglecting broader public interests. As one observer (Rydell, 1984, pp. 183–84) has described public involvement, "What thus begins as a grand design . . . often becomes an exercise in day-to-day bargaining where organized groups struggle to maximize their own vested interests often at the expense of broader social objectives." The blame does not lie entirely with those external groups either. According to one analysis (MacNair, Caldwell, and Pollane, 1983, p. 52), weaker governmental agencies may use public involvement to strengthen their position: "Public agencies avoid citizens if their position is strong, in order to maintain organizational stability. Relatively powerless agencies, however, are more likely to risk close alliance with their citizen participants in an effort to promote a stronger constituency."

In the end, the governmental process can become more fragmented as public involvement increases the number of groups and agencies pursuing special interests, without encouraging any new advocacy of broader public interests.

A New View: A Practical Theory of Public Involvement

These accumulated complaints pose a serious challenge to the theoretical case for public involvement articulated by the new public administration. Yet, far from cohering as a theoretical alternative to that perspective, the complaints only point to the earlier theory's flaws. A true alternative theory has yet to be developed.

Such a theory must combine the several perspectives just described, resolving their disagreements to the extent possible. The theory must also reflect a more balanced and realistic view of public involvement, accommodating both the enduring philosophical principles of earlier managerial theories and the practical concerns of public administrators. An alternative theory must also embody a contingent view of public involvement. Many of the disagreements about the virtues or sins of public involvement could be resolved by seeing its value as varying by situation. The point may seem obvious, but contributors to the literature on public involvement have largely neglected questions of when and how involvement is more or less appropriate. A new theory should define those contingencies.

The combination of a balanced perspective on what can realistically be expected from public involvement and a contingent perspective on how those expectations should vary according to the situation should result in a theory that has much more practical value for public managers than either the pure enthusiasm of the proponents of public involvement or the skepticism of its critics. At the same time, the joining of philosophy and practicality in one theory should also help managers to see the everyday practice of public involvement as consistent with how they think about their work in general.

The Balanced Perspective

The areas of agreement between the earlier perspectives are many. First, even the severest critics of public involvement agree on the desirability of involving the public in the managerial process, reflecting a general recognition that effective organizations require good communication from the bottom up as well as from the top down. Illustrative of this agreement, the theoretical consensus that public involvement is necessary is one of the few points of concurrence between the otherwise sharply contrasting market and communitarian approaches to contemporary governance. Communitarian thinkers emphasize group or community choices, while market theorists emphasize individual choice, but both camps agree on the need for more citizen participation in governance (see, for example, Lan and Rosenbloom, 1992).

Most critics would also probably accept Cooper's (1984) assertion that working for citizens, as, in a sense, "professional citizens," is an ethical obligation of public managers. Even Wilson (1887, p. 21), as he made the original argument for separating politics and administration, recognized the importance of public scrutiny of administration: "But, as superintending the greater forces of formative policy like in politics and in administration, public criticism is altogether safe and beneficent, altogether indispensable."

Nor do the communitarian and market perspectives differ entirely on the particulars of public involvement. Rather, arguments for public involvement emphasize mostly the potential benefits, while arguments against emphasize the possible costs. A balanced theory of public involvement must recognize both.

A first step in that direction is to recognize, as the critics contend, that meaningful public involvement is not easily achieved. Citizens are not easily persuaded to participate, and it is especially difficult to engage a representative cross section of citizens in any involvement. Yet even if significant numbers of citizens are persuaded to participate, the difficulties do not necessarily ease. As critics have observed, citizens and administrators are likely to distrust each other, at least at first. Administrators will initially question the representativeness of citizen participants: Do these people truly represent the people I need to hear from? Citizens for their part may question the motives of administrators: Do they really want my opinion, or are they only trying to sell me something?

Getting past this distrust takes time. The evidence suggests that both sides, public administrators and citizens, often undergo an unplanned, ad hoc, on-the-job learning process before public involvement brings any benefits. As Cole (1981, p. 58) concluded from a study of successful citizen involvement in community health organizations: "All of the programs experienced certain periods in which client involvement did not appear to be so effective. In fact, a common developmental cycle was evident, the stages of which seemed to progress from 'initial optimism' to 'confrontation and deadlock' to 'accommodation' to 'productive decision-making.'"

Yet, as Cole's description implies, the difficulties of the learning process need not persist; public involvement can become a positive experience for both public administrators and citizens.

Thinking in terms of a learning process helps to resolve the contrasting characterizations of public involvement as either unpleasant and emotionally draining or supportive and protective of administrators. Both characterizations may be accurate, but at different phases in the process. Unpleasantness is more likely to be experienced early, such as in the confrontation and deadlock phase, but should dissipate if the process progresses toward accommodation and productive decision making, when the two sides may become mutually supportive.

Advocates and skeptics can probably also agree that decision making with public involvement usually requires more time than without, even after the learning process is complete. Negotiating with multiple parties takes time. What critics overlook, however, is that the additional time spent on decision making can save time later. The time public managers spend on involving more actors in decision making can reduce the time necessary for implementation. The various actors, by virtue of being involved in the initial decisions, are more likely to support and even to expedite the implementation.

Other benefits may also be realized if the learning process is successfully completed. For administrators, those benefits can include better information on service needs, more services for the dollar, and better feelings about their work. For citizens, the gains can include services better suited to their needs, a more accessible and responsive public bureaucracy, and more positive feelings about themselves and government (for example, Yin and Yates, 1974).

The Contingent Perspective

A balanced perspective cannot accommodate all of the disagreements about public involvement. Public involvement cannot be described as, for example, both enhancing governmental effectiveness and compromising important public quality standards. These and other contrasting views can be accommodated only by adding a contingent perspective, which sees the merits of public involvement as varying by situation.

Take, for example, the contrasting perspectives on the costs of the new public involvement. Does this involvement result in more costs for administrators and their agencies, or is it instead a means for saving money? The answer may be contingent upon when and how administrators involve the public. It is true, as critics of involvement contend, that citizens may request changes that add to program costs, but program planners sometimes invite those costs by waiting too long before seeking citizen opinions. Opinions too often are solicited *after* detailed program plans are formulated, when changes can be accommodated only by adding costly embellishments. Similarly, agencies may be able to utilize citizen assistance to increase service levels without increasing costs, but the value of that assistance probably varies by service area (see Ahlbrandt and Sumka, 1983).

Consider also the disagreements about specific techniques of public involvement, such as public hearings. These hearings have been praised by Kihl (1985, pp. 198–199) as valuable for both managers and citizens, but condemned by Checkoway (1981, p. 571) as a vehicle only "to satisfy minimum legal requirements for citizen participation." Rather than either observer being wrong, it may be that public hearings work in some circumstances but not in others.

A contingent perspective is probably what most critics have been seeking. That goal is implicit, for example, in Cleveland's (1975, p. 6) advice to public managers: "The wise leader will not make a principle out of openness, or secrecy either." Few proponents of public involvement would argue the point.

The challenge is to articulate the specifics of a contingent perspective, to answer the questions one critic (Cupps, 1977, p. 484) posed of "how much public participation, in what form, under what circumstances, and with what impact on public policies and administration." It is here that critics and proponents alike have stumbled. The specifics of this perspective cannot be easily or quickly defined. To do so is, in essence, the task of the remainder of this book, beginning with the next chapter.

For the moment, the lesson of this chapter is that public managers, if they have not already done so, must change how they think about their work. They must internalize a view of public management that recognizes the need for public involvement in the managerial process. Contemporary public management requires too many important decisions for managers to continue to expect either a clear separation of politics and administration or a strictly top-down, hierarchical flow of influence. Managers must recognize the blurring of politics and administration and the increasingly multidirectional—alternately top-down, bottom-up, and lateral—flow of influence. They must also recognize the necessity of public involvement implied by this different perspective.

At the same time, managers should not be naively optimistic about the potential of public involvement. It can bring important gains, but it also carries serious risks. Maximizing the former and minimizing the latter requires taking a contingent perspective, viewing public involvement as desirable to varying degrees and in varying forms depending on the situation.

Chapter Three

First Steps in
Public Participation

The first task of the public manager in any public involvement process is to decide the degree of involvement. Should the public be involved at all? If so, how extensive should that involvement be, and how much authority should be shared with the public?

The right answers to those questions vary by issue because the trade-off between the benefits and the costs of public involvement varies by issue. Rather than being uniformly desirable or undesirable, public involvement is more desirable for some issues than for others. Consequently, the public manager's task is to determine that desirability as issues arise and then to involve the public appropriately. This chapter and the next two chapters focus on how public managers can make those determinations.

Determinations about citizen participation can be made by using the Effective Decision Model of Public Involvement. This model is based on a theory borrowed from the literature on small-group decision making (Vroom and Yetton, 1973; Vroom and Jago, 1988) and then adapted and empirically tested for issues of public involvement. The Effective Decision Model embodies guidelines designed to assist managers in deciding how much to involve the public in making any given decision. This chapter explains the model and illustrates its application to situations in which limited or no public involvement is desirable. Chapters Four and Five examine the model's recommendations for situations in which more extensive involvement is needed.

The Core Theory

The desirability of public involvement depends primarily on the relative need for quality versus the need for acceptability in an eventual decision. Some public issues embody greater needs for quality, that is, for consistency with professional standards, legislative mandates, budgetary constraints, and the like. Other issues carry greater needs for acceptability, for public acceptance of or compliance with any decision. Where the needs for quality are greater, there is less need to involve the public. Where, on the other hand, the needs for acceptability are greater, the need to involve the public and to share decision-making authority will be greater. Where both needs are substantial, there will be competing needs for public involvement and for constraints on that involvement.

An extensive literature on how managers should involve *subordinates* in making decisions argues that the determination should hinge on the same competition between quality and acceptability (see, for example, Field, 1979). Summarizing that literature, Vroom and Yetton (1973) proposed a theory to help managers decide how much to involve subordinates in decision making, a theory since developed further by Vroom and Jago (1988). The theory holds promise for also explaining when different degrees of public involvement are desirable. This promise rests on several factors. First, the principal variables in the theory are the same concepts that are central to questions of public involvement. The dependent variable is "decision and organizational effectiveness" (Field, 1979, p. 249), that is, the effectiveness of the decision and of the organization as a consequence of the decision. Public managers seek that same effectiveness in their decisions about involving the public. To explain the impact of involvement on effectiveness, the theory attempts to resolve the tension between decision quality and decision acceptability that also dominates debates about public involvement (see Cleveland, 1975; Cupps, 1977; Nelkin, 1984). Through its concern with acceptability, the theory can also address the questions of responsiveness and legitimacy that are so important in issues of public policy and public management.

Second, the available evidence suggests that the theory works in its original private-sector context (see Vroom and Yetton, 1973; Vroom, 1976; Vroom and Jago, 1978). Even one of the theory's early critics eventually concluded that "evidence has accumulated that managers should be aware of the [Vroom and Yetton] normative model and its potential use in decision making" (Field, 1982, p. 532). Given this evidence of validity for the private sector, the theory merits examination by the public sector.

Vroom and Yetton (1973, p. 40) themselves implied that the theory could work as effectively with publics as it appears to work with subordinates. They argued that the relevant "group" for the theory is "that set of persons or their representatives who are potentially affected by the decision," a definition that fits publics as easily as subordinates.

The Vroom-Yetton theory does require adaptation to recognize the special nature of public sector and public involvement issues. These issues are in some ways more complicated in that more time must be given to defining the relevant publics, which can be more numerous and diffuse than the relevant subordinates (see Chapter Four). In other respects, however, public sector issues prove less complicated, permitting some simplification of the model, as explained later in this chapter and in Chapter Five.

Use of the model by public managers may improve the effectiveness of eventual decisions. The model's predictive power was tested through a reanalysis of forty governmental decisions made with varying degrees of public involvement (for an explanation of the methodology and findings, see Appendix A). Consistency with the model's recommendations proved the best predictor of the effectiveness of those decisions (see also Thomas, 1990, 1993).

A Model for Decision Making

To use the Effective Decision Model, the manager must first recognize the situations in which a decision may be made on a matter of public policy, program implementation, or service delivery.
That characterization encompasses at least these situations in
which the model can be employed to assess the desirability of public involvement:

1. A manager must plan the administration of a new program of
   policy formulated by elected superiors or by a higher level of
   government.

2. A problem perceived by the manager or by the manager's
   elected superiors raises the possibility of modifying an existing
   program or developing a new program.

3. Some segment of the public requests governmental action on
   a perceived problem, and the manager is asked or chooses to
   assist in determining possible action.

The first step managers should take toward an effective decision
is to be alert to the possibility of any of these situations arising, and
then to be ready to initiate action. The case reanalysis showed
clearly that effective decisions—decisions viewed as more effective
by both managers *and* the public—were more often reached when
managers initiated action. Decision effectiveness was lower for those
issues that originated elsewhere, such as with a manager's elected
superior or a higher level of government, and lowest for issues that
originated in the external environment, such as with citizen groups.
Initiating issues presumably gives managers more ability to guide
their development and, in the process, to assert agency priorities.
Issues that are forced on the manager by others may already be
defined in a manner that could threaten those priorities.

In most of these situations, managers have at least some choice
about how to involve the public. Only rarely do statutory require-

ments or orders from elected superiors stipulate exactly how, if at all, the public is to be involved. In almost all of the cases in the reanalysis, for example, the manager/decision maker could influence the decision about how to involve the public, exercising exclusive authority over that decision in 50 percent of the cases and sharing that authority, usually with elected officials, in an additional 43 percent. The choice for the manager is sometimes whether to invite public involvement at all; more often, however, public involvement may be required, but it is left to the manager to determine how, when, and to what extent to seek that involvement.

Using the Effective Decision Model, the manager can choose between three general options: (1) autocratic or autonomous decision making, with no public involvement or influence; (2) consultative decision making, with a limited but significant public role; and (3) public decision making, with the extensive influence of a decision made jointly by the manager and the public. Two of these options can be further broadened to produce a total of five decision-making approaches, varying in their extent of public involvement and influence:

1. *Autonomous managerial decision.* The manager solves the problem or makes the decision alone without public involvement.

2. *Modified autonomous managerial decision.* The manager seeks information from segments of the public, but decides alone in a manner that may or may not reflect group influence.

3. *Segmented public consultation.* The manager shares the problem separately with segments of the public, getting ideas and suggestions, then makes a decision that reflects group influence.

4. *Unitary public consultation.* The manager shares the problem with the public as a single assembled group, getting ideas and suggestions, then makes a decision that reflects group influence. (This approach requires only that all members of the public have the opportunity to be involved, such as in

well-publicized public hearings, not that everyone actually participate.)

5. *Public decision.* The manager shares the problem with the assembled public, and together the manager and the public attempt to reach agreement on a solution.

As this limited range implies, some choices are *not* available to the manager. First, contrary to the practice of some public officials, public involvement does not include the option of only consulting the public after a decision has been made. Talking with the public at that point does not constitute true involvement; the public is being informed rather than participating in making a decision. Simply informing the public of a decision can be entirely appropriate, but not if disguised as a form of public involvement to imply possible influence.

Second, underlying these options is the assumption that varying degrees of involvement equate with varying degrees of public influence; that is, the more extensive the involvement, the greater the public's influence over a decision. This equation is not logically necessary, since the public could be—and has been—extensively involved in decisions in which little or no influence was shared, but it is necessary in practice. With direct compensation seldom available to induce or reward involvement, other incentives are essential, and the promise of influence is usually a minimum. Obtaining a particular level of public involvement consequently requires offering a comparable degree of influence as incentive. Only the limited involvement of a "modified autonomous" approach—in which, for example, the public may only be asked questions in a phone survey—may be invited without the promise of influence.

Managers who ignore this need, particularly by seeking involvement greater than the influence they are willing to share, risk a failed public involvement process. The public may either recognize the lack of incentives and participate less than desired, or participate as desired but then become frustrated and disenchanted with the limited opportunity for influence. Such participants will think carefully before responding to a future call for public involvement.

This limited range of five approaches may be preferable to the larger number of options suggested elsewhere. For example, Arnstein's (1969) well-known "ladder of citizen participation" has eight "rungs," but several (for example, "manipulation") represent involvement without influence. In addition, as explained in Chapters Six and Seven, these five options can be expanded to a broader choice among specific mechanisms of public involvement.

The Characteristics of Issues

To make an appropriate choice among the five approaches, the manager must ask a series of seven questions about the characteristics of the issue at hand:

1. What are the quality requirements that must be incorporated in any decision?

2. Do I have sufficient information to make a high quality decision?

3. Is the problem structured such that alternative solutions are not open to redefinition?

4. Is public acceptance of the decision critical to effective implementation? If so, is that acceptance reasonably certain if the manager decides alone?

5. Who is the relevant public? And, does that public consist of an organized group, more than one organized group, an unorganized public, or some combination of the three?

6. Does the relevant public share the agency goals to be obtained in solving the problem?

7. Is there likely to be conflict within the public on the preferred solution?

The questions are designed to define the relative needs for quality and acceptability in any decision, and should be asked in any situation in which public involvement is possible, preferably *before* any action is taken. Combining the answers to all of the questions will suggest if and how the public should be involved. The first four questions are explained in this chapter.

The Quality Constraints

The first three questions inquire about the quality constraints on an eventual solution.

1. What are the quality requirements that must be incorporated in any decision?

"Quality requirements" refer to almost any policy or managerial constraint on the nature of the eventual decision (Vroom and Yetton, 1973, pp. 21–22), such as (1) technical constraints that limit which solutions can be considered (as when experience has shown that a particular solution does not work); (2) regulatory constraints on elements that must be included in any solution; and (3) budgetary constraints on how much money can be spent on a solution. Quality requirements could include:

• Safety and effectiveness in the regulation of drugs by the Food and Drug Administration (Friedman, 1978)
• A location that would "encourage greater use of mass transit" while also minimizing "adverse impacts on traffic congestion" in the planning to build an extension of a mass transit line (McCarthy and Howitt, 1984, pp. 275, 284)

Any such requirements may provide grounds for limiting public involvement in order to protect quality.

The problems that confront public managers invariably bring

quality requirements, ranging from a budget ceiling at the minimum to a precise set of regulations at the maximum. Constraints are a way of life in the highly controlled and regulated public sector. Fearing the public wrath that can follow even the appearance of malfeasance, policy makers circumscribe managers' discretion with an "array of laws, procedures, and norms intended to closely control their behavior" (Whorton and Worthley, 1983, p. 126). As a consequence, the first task in contemplating public involvement is to identify an issue's quality requirements.

That can be difficult. Some quality requirements may have been assumed for so long that their importance is no longer consciously recognized. The manager may become aware of such requirements only when challenged by the public during an involvement process, and at that point, imposing new constraints on the authority of that involvement could anger participants. In addition, managers can have difficulty distinguishing a true quality requirement from what is only a personal preference. Is this requirement really necessary, a manager may wonder, or is it only my personal bias? Accurate identification of quality requirements in advance of public involvement does not close the issue, however. Requirements could change during decision making if new legislation is passed or a budget crisis develops unexpectedly; or citizens might question the necessity of particular requirements, contending that public officials have cloaked their personal preferences in the more impressive garb of quality requirements (see Petersen, 1984, p. 3).

These difficulties may not be as great as the difficulties that might arise if the question about quality requirements is *not* asked and answered at the outset. A manager who invites public involvement without first contemplating these requirements endangers legitimate quality considerations by not declaring that they must be respected. Although the manager can belatedly state quality requirements, that delay could alienate citizens who have assumed that their authority was broader. Advance specification of quality requirements does not assure either their preservation or the satisfaction of citizen participants, but it makes both outcomes more likely.

The second question about quality constraints that managers must ask is about the need for information to use in making the decision:

2. Do I have sufficient information to make a high quality decision?

The need for information to enhance quality usually calls for more involvement, not less. A negative answer gives the manager cause to turn to citizens as a source for information (Vroom and Yetton, 1973, pp. 23–24).

Several kinds of information might be needed. First, information may be desired on how well a decision will work in the field. A decision on a neighborhood law enforcement program might benefit from information on when and where residents perceive enforcement problems to be most acute. Second, information may be needed on public preferences, on what kinds of solutions potential consumers of the program prefer. That information can help in avoiding the offering of unnecessary or unacceptable services. Third, the manager may need technical information on a problem or on possible solutions. Only in this latter case might the need for information not call for more public involvement, although the public can sometimes be helpful here, too.

Problem structure represents a third possible quality constraint. In the private sector, according to Vroom and Yetton (1973, p. 25), structure means that the manager knows the alternatives and how to evaluate them. In the public sector, by contrast, structure usually means only that the choice about how to address the problem has been reduced to a limited range of possible solutions, independent of what is known about how to evaluate the solutions. Adequate information is not a necessary prerequisite for problem structure in political environments. The question managers need to ask is:

3. Is the problem structured such that alternative solutions are not open to redefinition?

Many public sector issues eventually come down to such a forced choice between two or a few alternatives.

Problem structure may provide grounds for limiting the scope of public involvement. Protecting that structure may require either avoiding involvement entirely or limiting the public's influence to a choice between alternatives. In the latter case, the public's involvement must be prefaced with an explanation of how the structure limits the decision latitude.

Even with that advance explanation, public involvement in debating structured problems can prove difficult for the manager and a threat to decision effectiveness. At one extreme, citizens may view a limited choice between already-defined alternatives as not warranting expenditure of their time, and so decline the invitation to become involved. At the other extreme, citizens may reject the structure and in so doing veto any governmental action. When asked to aid in choices about "either-or" sitings of "LULUs" (locally undesirable land uses), for example, the public has frequently responded with a flat "no" or the loud "NIMBY" cry of "not in my backyard!"

To avoid these hazards, managers should hesitate before defining problems as structured. The manager should carefully consider whether any apparent structure could be waived, thereby broadening the choice available to the public. Better yet, the manager should invite public involvement before the problem becomes structured. Many problems in which the public should be involved can be broached before they become structured as the "yes-no" or "all-or-none" choices that are so resistant to compromise.

Even as they attempt to answer these questions *before* involving the public, public managers often need to reconsider the answers as the result of public involvement. The perspective of citizens can clarify managers' thinking, as illustrated by the recent experience of the U.S. Forest Service described in Case 3.1 (adapted from Manring, 1993).

———•———

Case 3.1

Involving the Public in Defining Quality Constraints: Negotiations with the Forest Service

The Forest Service began experimenting in the early 1980s with nontraditional techniques for involving the public in resolving environmental disputes. Spurred by the success of these efforts in combination with a growing number of unresolved disputes, the Service in 1988 revised its procedures to increase the use of negotiations for resolving appeals of forest plans (Manring, 1993, p. 345). Judging from in-depth interviews with Forest Service personnel, the negotiation approach proved to be a generally positive change; the benefits included unanticipated assistance in redefining quality requirements and information needs.

To begin with, questioning from representatives of the public often forced Service personnel to reconsider whether stated quality requirements and problem structure were truly essential. Some Service officials admitted to confusing "conventional management practice" with science-based quality requirements or problem structure. The conventional practices were usually based on science, but often were not the only possible approach consistent with that science. The practice of clear-cutting is illustrative.

Clear-cutting has been the dominant timber harvesting method for so long that it has become synonymous with scientific resource management in the eyes of many agency officials. Looking through the familiar lens of tradition, agency officials may think that their decision space is rather narrow, with little latitude for change. Consequently, modifications in management practices advocated during negotiations may be perceived as a threat. For example, when environmental appellants urged the Forest Service to adopt timber harvest practices other than clear-cutting, agency officials wedded to tradition often thought that they were being asked to step outside the boundaries of the acceptable decision space (p. 352). In reality, clear-cutting was not required by any good scientific rationale. Negotiations forced Forest Service staff to recognize that fact without compromising the scientific basis of policies: "Although environmental appellants have pressured Forest Service officials to modify conventional management practices, during negotiations the scientific basis of those decisions has remained intact" (p. 352).

Questioning from the public forced Forest Service personnel to provide better substantiation for other supposedly scientifically based quality requirements and problem structure as well. The public in this case included many knowledgeable groups: "Several national environmental interest groups such as the Wilderness Society, Sierra Club and Audubon Society are known for their exhaustive, detailed analyses of forest plans. Industry groups that include representatives of timber harvesting and forest products industries also have carefully scrutinized forest plans to determine how their own interests will be affected" (p. 349). To negotiate with those groups, as one Forest Service negotiator said, "You better know what you're talking about or you're going to get embarrassed" (p. 349).

Involving public groups in these negotiations also improved the information base for decision making. In addition to providing information on consumer preferences, those groups provided useful scientific information. Indeed, to keep pace with those groups, Forest Service "officials have been pushed to incorporate the most current information in their discussions and analyses." As a result, Service officials "found that negotiating appeals also strengthened the scientific basis of decisions by broadening the knowledge base upon which decisions were made" (p. 349).

Public involvement may often lead managers to redefine quality requirements, problem structure, and information needs. Yet managers should not simply postpone that redefinition for this process. The better strategy, as in the Forest Service case, is to take a preliminary definition to the public, and to reconsider it as public involvement suggests is necessary.

───◆───

Needs for Acceptability

Once the core needs for quality are defined, questions of acceptability become paramount. The principal reason for involving the public in decision making is to increase acceptance of the decision, especially when implementation hinges on that acceptance. Involvement increases the likelihood of public acceptance and of successful implementation by nurturing citizen "ownership" of the decision.

Successful implementation in the public sector means more than simply completing physical implementation and having a program operating. Strident public objections that persist may remain salient in the highly politicized environment of government, and may threaten the decision or even the decision maker. It may not be sufficient, for example, to have successfully opened a halfway house for drug offenders if nearby homeowners continue to object to its presence. Successful implementation in the public sector requires both completion of physical implementation and a lack of subsequent public outcry.

Involvement is not necessary in all situations in which implementation requires public acceptance. Citizens sometimes view the anticipated outcome of a decision as so desirable that they will accept a decision without being involved. For instance, decisions that promise new jobs for declining cities may be accepted without public involvement because citizens are desperate for economic growth. Consequently, the manager must ask a two-part question about the need for citizen acceptance:

4. *Is public acceptance of the decision critical to effective implementation? If so, is that acceptance reasonably certain if the manager decides alone?*

A negative answer to the first part of the question or an affirmative answer to the second part reduces or eliminates the need for public involvement. Involvement can unnecessarily complicate matters if acceptance is not needed or is already assured. On the other hand, managers should be cautious about assuming acceptance without involvement. Even the residents of declining cities have sometimes rejected economic development proposals despite the promise of new jobs (see Fox, 1985).

Initial Applications of the Model

After asking the first four questions, the manager can make an initial judgment on whether public involvement is necessary by tracing the answers through the first part of the Effective Decision Model decision tree, shown in Figure 3.1. With many issues, the answers will already indicate that the manager should decide alone, taking the autonomous managerial approach, or with only the limited involvement of the modified autonomous managerial approach.

Using the Autonomous Managerial Approach

The answers to the first four questions may indicate that the public should *not* be involved because quality concerns are controlling. That is, the decision must respect quality requirements and perhaps problem structure, and neither information nor acceptance is needed from the public. If the public can neither contribute to nor gain from involvement and the manager has much to protect, the decision should probably be made in-house, independent of the public.

Figure 3.1. The Effective Decision Model
of Public Involvement: First Steps.

1	2	3	4
What are the quality requirements?	Do I have sufficient information?	Is the problem structured?	Is public acceptance necessary for implementation and unlikely without involvement?

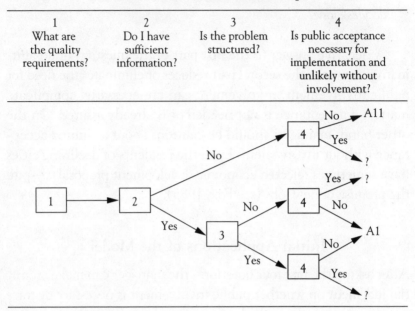

Key: A1 = Autonomous managerial decision
    A11 = Modified autonomous managerial decision

Soliciting involvement on such issues is risky as well as unnecessary. These risks became realities in the Environmental Protection Agency's (EPA) experience with water quality planning in two
Texas communities, as profiled in Case 3.2 (adapted from Plumlee,
Starling, and Kramer, 1985).

————•————

Case 3.2

Citizen Participation in Water Quality Planning

As part of its charge to improve water quality, in the late 1970s the
Environmental Protection Agency undertook water quality planning in a number of communities around the country. These efforts
included two Texas communities.

Required by law to encourage citizen participation in this planning, EPA staff chose to form citizen advisory committees in both communities as the core of an elaborate participation process. Approximately fifty people were named to each committee. Members were selected to "reflect a broad sampling of the relevant publics" and included "public officials, those with economic interests, the general public, and representatives of the 'public interest.'" Committee procedures were also carefully planned to insure "a substantial degree of citizen participation" (Plumlee, Starling, and Kramer, 1985, p. 460).

But was such an elaborate participation process really desirable? A close analysis of the issues at stake in the planning suggests it was not. To begin with, the quality requirements were extensive. "It is unlikely . . . that the constraints on the . . . process would have allowed for any substantial deviation from what was deemed technically or economically feasible" (pp. 463–465). The purview of the planning was also severely circumscribed since, consistent with congressional wishes, the EPA required that local planning efforts "concern themselves exclusively with non-point source problems" of water quality (p. 464). There was no latitude to redefine the problem to include the issues of greatest interest at the Texas sites: point source pollution concerns related to a local creek at one site, and water *quantity* concerns due to shortages at the other site.

Nor were the needs for information, acceptability, or both sufficient to justify extensive public involvement. The EPA's expressed need for information—"to test public reaction to and public comprehension of rather technical policy proposals"—appeared to be a rhetorical disguise for an interest in performing the "educative function" of "making the public aware of . . . the need for water quality planning." There was no evidence that new information could have changed program plans; those plans were already largely defined by technical and economic constraints. Nor was there any apparent need for involvement as a means to facilitate implementation. Implementation of the plans either did not require citizen acceptance, or, if acceptance was necessary, it probably could have been assumed without public involvement (pp. 462–463).

Public managers sometimes face this situation—a program so rigidly constrained by law and so lacking in latitude for outside influence that public involvement makes no sense. These are the problems managers should keep to themselves, resolving them through the autonomous managerial approach. When EPA planners instead attempted extensive consultation by establishing advisory committees, the results were predictably unsatisfactory. For the EPA, the decision-making process became unnecessarily complicated, contributing to "lengthy delays" in the planning process at the Texas sites. For the citizens who became involved, the lack of a significant role created frustration and disenchantment, as illustrated by the many citizen participants who became "increasingly dispirited or angry." For both sides, the process seemed not worth the effort: "In one way or another every participant . . . indicated that the 208 planning process had been ineffective" (pp. 466–468).

Using the Modified Autonomous Managerial Approach

As the EPA case illustrates, public managers sometimes face legal requirements to involve the public in situations for which the Effective Decision Model recommends no involvement (that is, there are no apparent needs for either public information or acceptability). The best choice then is to pursue the least public involvement permissible, aiming to satisfy legal requirements without falsely raising public expectations by inviting more participation than is needed or justified. Had that advice been followed in the Texas case, the EPA might have used public hearings rather than building an elaborate advisory committee structure. In taking such an approach, the manager chooses the modified autonomous managerial approach over an entirely autonomous approach. That is, the manager seeks information from segments of the public, but decides alone in a manner which may or may not reflect group influence.

Such an approach is also recommended by the Effective Decision Model when information, but not acceptance, is needed from the public. Acceptance either is not critical for implementation or, if critical, is reasonably certain if the manager decides alone. Needing only information, the manager need neither involve the public extensively nor share much influence. The utility of the modified autonomous approach under such circumstances is suggested by the decision making that led to the building of a nuclear power plant in Vermont, as detailed in Case 3.3 (adapted from Ebbin and Kasper, 1974).

-----•-----

Case 3.3

Constructing the Vermont Nuclear Power Station

On November 30, 1966, the Vermont Nuclear Power Corporation applied to the Atomic Energy Commission (AEC) for permission to build a nuclear power plant in a rural, largely undeveloped area near Vernon, Vermont. It was the AEC's responsibility to decide whether to grant that permission.

As in the EPA case, the AEC's decision would have to respect important quality requirements, including operation without "undue risk to the health and safety of the public" (Ebbin and Kasper, 1974, p. 92). In contrast to the EPA case, however, this decision was also constrained by problem structure (plant or no plant).

Public involvement was necessary as a consequence of two other characteristics of the issue. First, more information was needed on public preferences. Second, public involvement was legally required: "The AEC requires hearings in construction permit cases and permits interested parties to intervene in these hearings" (p. 92).

Public acceptance, however, could be assumed without involvement. Although the same issue would arouse broad public opposition only a few years later, there was "no organized citizen opposition" in 1967. Instead, area residents tended to view the proposed plan as "progress" for the area (p. 92).

Here was a situation that arises occasionally: a problem with many constraints, no need for acceptance, but a need for information from the public and a legal requirement for public involvement. This is the ideal situation for using the modified autonomous decision-making approach.

The AEC utilized that approach through a series of four public hearings to which the public was invited but not strongly encouraged to attend. The results were generally positive—in the short term anyway—as the plant was successfully constructed and few parties voiced dissatisfaction with the decision-making process (pp. 94–95).

The modified autonomous approach can also be useful as a first step in a public involvement process that eventually requires other steps. The information the manager obtains through this approach may help to resolve uncertainty about a need for public acceptance requiring public involvement. Should such a need become evident, the manager must answer some additional questions, which will be discussed in Chapters Four and Five.

Public managers should be cautious about using either the autonomous or modified autonomous approach to decision making. Many, if not most, issues include the need for public acceptance if decisions are to be successfully implemented. Fully 91 percent of the cases included in the reanalysis, for example, brought such a need. Although it probably overstates the actual proportion of public management decisions likely to require public acceptance, that figure suggests that many managerial decisions should be resolved with more participation than a modified autonomous managerial approach implies. Before resolving these issues, the manager must consider the nature of the public, the subject of the next chapter.

Chapter Four

Defining the Relevant Publics

Whenever public involvement becomes necessary as a means to obtain public acceptance, public managers must attempt to define which groups and individuals may be interested in the issue and to gain a sense of the opinions they hold. Despite being rooted in dissatisfaction with how assessments of the public were made in the past, the new public involvement did not emerge with ready-made instructions for managers on how to produce better assessments. Nor does the original Vroom-Yetton model, given its original focus on the more easily defined "subordinates," provide the necessary guidance. This chapter offers such guidelines within the context of the Effective Decision Model.

In addition to defining the relevant groups, managers must make judgments, often as opinions are voiced in public deliberations, about who speaks for the public or, in any event, who represents whom. They must also consider what other actors, such as people from other levels or units of government, have a stake in the issue sufficient to require their involvement. Without an ability to make good judgments on these matters, public managers will not know either who to involve or what opinions to heed in formulating a possible solution.

Who Are the Relevant Publics?

Following the premises of the Effective Decision Model, the relevant publics on a given issue include all organized and unorganized groups of citizens or citizen representatives who (a) could provide information, about consumer preferences, for example, useful in resolving the issue, or (b) could affect the ability to implement a decision by accepting or facilitating implementation. These two criteria can be useful to public managers, and at the same time, also meet the needs of the public. Given the many demands on their time and resources, most citizens prefer not to be involved in most public decisions. The twin criteria of relevant information and implementation assistance should identify the segments of the public potentially interested. Citizens usually want to be involved only when they have strong feelings on an issue or when a decision will affect them directly. In broader democratic terms, these two criteria point to the quarters where the consent of the governed should be sought.

The relevant publics can consist of a wide array of groups, including traditional interest groups, such as business lobbies, labor unions, and program beneficiaries, as well as consumer and environmental groups, other public interest groups, residential groups (either organized homeowners associations or unorganized residents who are geographically targeted by a decision), and advisory committees that include representatives of any of these other groups. It can also include heretofore unorganized groups that may share an interest in a particular issue. In the middle and late 1960s, for example, many public issues aroused opposition from embryonic but unorganized environmental groups. Public managers should consider all of these possible publics in attempting to answer a two-part question:

5. *Who is the relevant public? And, does that public consist of an organized group, more than one organized group, an unorganized public, or some combination of the three?*

In addition to indicating *whose* involvement might be sought, the answer to this question carries implications for *how* involvement should be structured. The desirable structures vary greatly depending on the number of groups in the relevant public and their degree of organization. This issue is explored in detail in Chapters Six and Seven, but a few examples here may be useful.

If the relevant public consists of only one organized group, such as an organization of neighborhood residents, that group's regular meetings might be used as the arena for public involvement, with the group's communication channels used to publicize the opportunity. Those meetings might be supplemented by informal conversations with group leaders.

Regular group meetings can still be used for public involvement when the relevant public is comprised of two or more organized groups, but the manager must be prepared for the possibility of different meetings producing different recommendations. A better alternative may be to appoint an advisory committee representing all groups and empowered to develop a single recommendation.

The task grows more complicated when the relevant public is unorganized. There is no obvious arena for involving an unorganized public, nor any established communication channels for reaching its members. It is left to the manager to select an arena, such as a public hearing, and to assure adequate publicity of its availability.

Perhaps the most common situation finds the public manager faced with a complex public including both organized and unorganized groups. With the dramatic growth in the number of citizen groups in recent decades (see Walker, 1983), more than one organized group may be interested in many or most issues. Yet, large unorganized publics remain unrepresented on many issues; and even when an organized group is representative, the manager may not know that beforehand. Consequently, public managers commonly find that the relevant public on a given issue includes both organized groups and unorganized publics, as in 64 percent of the cases examined in the reanalysis discussed in Chapter Three and Appendix A.

A complex public poses a dilemma for the manager. Ignoring an organized group to solicit comments from a broader public could risk turning the group against the manager, perhaps endangering implementation of any decision. Still, the risks of ignoring an as yet unorganized public are probably greater, since implementation of a decision could grind to a halt if and when that public eventually recognizes its interest in the issue.

Goal Agreement Within the Publics

After identifying the relevant publics, public managers should attempt, in advance of any public involvement, to define the nature of public sentiment on the issue. A complete picture of the publics' opinions can develop only through actual public involvement, if then, but choosing how to pursue that involvement is easier if the manager can anticipate the broad contours of those feelings (Vroom and Yetton, 1973, pp. 29–30), especially with respect to what the agency sees as the goals for the issue (for example, legislative mandates or scientific standards). The first question to ask is:

6. *Does the relevant public share the agency goals to be obtained in solving the problem?*

The answer should affect how much decision-making authority will be shared with the public. Given a need for public acceptance of a decision, the manager should share some authority whatever the answer, but the manager who anticipates public agreement with the agency's goals has reason to share more authority. The manager who anticipates disagreement or who does not know what to anticipate will want to retain more authority to protect agency goals. In the former case, the manager might decide with the public, while in the latter, the manager might only consult them.

Finally, the manager will sometimes need to ask the following question (Vroom and Yetton, 1973, p. 30):

7. *Is there likely to be conflict within the public on the preferred solution?*

This question becomes relevant only when the public is *not* expected to share the agency's goals. Conflict within the public under these circumstances may call for more involvement in order to place some of the responsibility for resolving the conflict on the public, rather than placing all of it on the manager exclusively. The conflict might call for bringing the public together *as a single group*, as, say, in either an open public meeting or an advisory committee representing all segments of the public. By meeting as a single group, a divided public can become aware of its internal divisions, and so become more sympathetic to the plight of the manager, who must try to shape a decision acceptable to all.

Conversely, consulting with the public as a single group may not make sense if the segments are likely to *agree* with each other on their own goals, but to *disagree* with the agency's goals. To meet as a single group in this situation could build the public's sense of unity in opposition to the agency, undermining any managerial effort to assert agency goals. A better choice is to hold a series of meetings, each with a different segment of the public.

Techniques for Defining the Relevant Publics

Getting accurate answers to these questions ordinarily requires a combination of techniques, including both top-down approaches directed by the manager and bottom-up approaches emanating from the public.

The Top-Down Approach

In the top-down approach, managers, assisted by staff, attempt to answer the questions in advance of any public involvement. Managers should begin by thinking broadly about what types of citizens are likely to be interested in the issue. Who is or might be directly affected? Available lists of organized groups might then be checked to identify groups representing those citizens. A rudimentary historical analysis might also be undertaken to identify groups that have previously shown interest in similar programs (see Freeman, 1984, p. 54). Brainstorming with agency personnel could elicit more ideas. Calls to key contacts in the community, itself a form of public involvement, may yield yet additional suggestions.

There is a risk of being overwhelmed by too many interests if the relevant publics are defined too broadly. As Freeman (1984, p. 190) warned businesses about involving their publics, "the distinction between important and nonimportant stakeholders must be drawn somewhere." The risk of being too *exclusive* in this initial definition is probably greater than the risk of being too *inclusive*, however. Public decisions may be threatened more by interested groups that were overlooked than by uninterested groups that were not. Exclusivity is more appropriately exercised at a later point, as in deciding which groups warrant representation on an advisory committee.

The manager should be especially careful not to overlook significant unorganized publics, that is, citizens who share an interest in the issue but lack formal organization. Managers sometimes become aware of these publics only at the last minute, too late for meaningful involvement, when the imminence of a project suddenly mobilizes residents of a targeted area. The costs of overlooking these groups can be substantial, as the state of Washington learned when it attempted to plan a new ferry landing for the town of Port Townsend, discussed in Case 4.1 (adapted from Talbot, 1983).

———•———

Case 4.1

Siting the Port Townsend Terminal, Part I

Port Townsend depends on ferry service as its principal route to mainland Washington. In 1972 the Department of Transportation for the state of Washington assumed responsibility for the ferry service after financial problems forced a private operator to abandon its service. Facing an increasingly heavy traffic flow, the department decided to purchase a new and larger ferry, which in turn created a need to find a new and larger ferry landing.

The procedure followed by the department's marine division for selecting the site for the new landing appeared in many ways to be exemplary. The division at the outset made explicit its quality requirements, including "needs for quick traffic movement, sufficient parking, and size," and a budget ceiling of $3 million (Talbot, 1983, pp. 86–87). Recognizing that implementation required community acceptance, the division also structured a decision-making process to share authority for site selection with a citizens advisory committee representing organized community interests appointed by city hall.

This procedure appeared at first to work well. By early 1976, "working with the mayor and city council of Port Townsend and a local ferry advisory committee, the marine division was ready to build a new terminal about a block south of the existing landing" (p. 81).

All that changed at a July 1976 town forum on the city's future: "When the question of the new ferry landing came up, several people, nobody remembers exactly how many, strongly objected to the new location" (p. 82). As discussions continued in the ensuing months, the marine division learned that the objections, rather than being isolated, reflected the sentiments of a growing segment of the town's population, a segment comprised of relatively new arrivals who had moved to Port Townsend for the "simplicity" and "beauty of its setting" (p. 82). Unlike the community's longtime residents, these newcomers were not much interested in the area's economic growth, and so did not favor site selection designed to maximize the development potential.

Until the ferry site issue arose, the newcomers were not organized. Due either to the recency of their arrival or to their disagreements with the town's traditional leaders, they had also not been included on the advisory committee appointed to work on the site selection. As a consequence, when the marine division used existing organized groups in the planning of the ferry site, the newcomers' objections were not heard. Their views surfaced only when the tentative site had been selected, too late to be accommodated in an easy compromise.

The marine division paid dearly for the oversight. There was first a frustrating wait, stretching from 1976 until the middle of 1978, as the opposing factions bickered over possible sites for the new ferry location (p. 84). Then, when the issue was finally resolved, the marine division's $3 million budget estimate doubled to an eventual estimated cost (as of 1982, when the contracts expired) of $6 million (p. 89).

———————

Latent groups often can be identified if a manager is thorough about the enterprise of identifying relevant publics. In the Port Townsend case, for example, the growing traffic flow might have served as a clue to the town's changing population. Any additional time spent on identifying unseen groups can be more than justified if the manager consequently averts the kinds of delays and cost overruns witnessed in Port Townsend.

Port Townsend's experience also suggests the limitations of the top-down approach to defining relevant publics. No matter how careful their efforts, public managers cannot always identify all relevant groups in advance. One group or another will frequently elude advance identification, only to emerge later as an important player in decision making.

The Bottom-Up Approach

To prepare for the possibility of the emergence of latent publics, public managers must also rely in part on a bottom-up approach for defining relevant publics. In this approach, the manager essentially lets the public define itself, revealing its nature during the process of public involvement. Every public involvement should include at least some bottom-up definition. If the nature of the public were clearly known in advance, public involvement would be superfluous.

In using this approach, the manager must let public involvement proceed and be sensitive to what it reveals. The manager, or others acting on the manager's behalf, should take care to observe what groups and interests emerge, as well as what opinions they hold, as public involvement unfolds. The manager need not be a passive observer. Managers frequently can structure opportunities for bottom-up definition, thus both facilitating the definition and ensuring smooth operation of the process. Needless to say, such steps should be designed neither to manipulate nor to distort this definition.

A manager might try, for example, to separate the initial definition process from the actual decision making. Public involvement might begin with a citizen survey, which could suggest how citizens feel about an issue without at the same time prompting calls for action on the part of one group or another. This approach should not distort or mute the expression of public opinion if appropriate forums are eventually provided for voicing those calls for action. A less formal approach to the same end would be for the manager to query key contacts about the nature of the relevant public (although key contacts do not always have a good reading on divisions of opinion in the public). Either approach, in any event, may help the manager to define the public without at the same time moving too rapidly toward a decision.

Managers will not always need or be able to achieve this kind of separation. Prior experience with an issue will frequently give managers enough confidence about the nature of the public to move into decision making without redefining the relevant public first. The manager may also have neither the time nor the resources (such as personnel and funds to conduct a survey) necessary for separating decision making from the definition of the public.

When the definition of the public and the decision making proceed in tandem, other steps may be necessary to assure that the relevant public arrives on schedule. Public meetings, for example, sometimes draw little response to a proposed project, but a significant public opposition may rapidly mobilize, as happened in Port Townsend, when the project moves into implementation. That kind of delayed mobilization is also a common occurrence with the siting of so-called "LULUs" ("locally undesirable land uses"), when citizens join in opposition after planners have settled on a specific neighborhood site for the LULU.

Public managers can reduce the likelihood of such problems by making the opportunities for public involvement accessible and attractive. Public meetings should be scheduled at convenient times and places; the schedule and the issues to be discussed should be given plenty of advance publicity; and the potential for public influence should be made explicit.

No technique carries a guarantee of pulling interested citizens from their homes, but using a combination of techniques increases the likelihood that interested groups will become involved early in project planning. Had these guidelines been followed in the Port Townsend case, the marine division might have planned an early meeting of the citizens advisory committee as a public hearing on the ferry landing issue. Extensive prior publicity might have attracted many of the community's newcomers, whose objections could then have been heard before a plan had been formulated. That effort could have been made within the same advisory committee structure, with the marine division thereby averting or reducing the substantial delays and cost overruns that eventually resulted.

Who Represents Whom?

The task of determining who represents whom is at least as challenging as defining the relevant publics. The strident voices that sometimes articulate widely shared opinions can also reflect only the isolated opinions of a small minority who try to achieve through volume what they lack in numbers. Similarly, voices too low to be heard over the din sometimes speak for the many.

There are no easy rules for making sense of these many voices. However, as the experience of administrators and council members in Cincinnati instructs, such judgments can be made by using a variety of techniques, as illustrated in Case 4.2 (adapted from Thomas, 1986).

Case 4.2

Assessing the Representativeness of Cincinnati's Community Councils

Working with neighborhood groups, as one Cincinnati official said, "you always have that awful question of who does this group of people really speak for" (Thomas, 1986, p. 97). Although supporters argue that neighborhood groups represent the public, the evidence indicates that these groups are often far from representative of their communities (see, for example, Cole, 1974).

That fact raised major problems for Cincinnati officials when they invited community council involvement in municipal policy making and implementation. To begin with, as one city council member reported, "The usual problem is how many people do they represent. You have some neighborhood groups that are very vocal, and you're surprised to find out later that there's a total of ten members in the group. That's a problem because you really don't have a good fix on how many people are actively involved" (Thomas, 1986, p. 97).

Alternatively, municipal officials sometimes must decide who to believe when more than one group claims to represent an area. The boundaries claimed by different groups sometimes partially or completely overlap. Dissenting voices in a community also may claim that the recognized community organization does not speak for the community. As one Cincinnati administrator recalled, "One of the community councils had a leader who was a bar owner. I used to get people coming up and whispering to me all the time [at public meetings], 'Don't pay any attention to that guy'" (p. 97).

Even when an administrator has determined who a particular group represents, that knowledge can quickly become obsolete. Given the volatile nature of neighborhood groups, a group may not represent tomorrow the same people it represents today. As a housing official observed, "You get a group which started and was very active. You still find yourself talking to them, but there's really nothing there anymore" (p. 97).

Most of Cincinnati's municipal administrators were well aware of these problems and unwilling to cast them aside quickly. Instead, they usually took the stance described by a planning official: "We assume they [the community groups] represent a number of people. We also assume they don't represent everybody." From there, as a city council member said, "You just have to guess and ask questions" (p. 98).

A good first question to ask is about the size of a group's membership. According to one administrator, "You get groups when you say, 'Write down the list of your members,' when they get past the fifth line, they start running out of names." The question of size may also be answered by observing the group's turnout at public meetings. For at least one administrator, the representative groups, or in any event, the groups he listened to, "are the ones that stand up on Wednesday afternoon in front of city council." Another technique is to observe group turnout across several meetings. As another administrator said, "Often you'll go through a couple of hearings before the true picture can be understood" (p. 98).

A different approach involves looking at a group's procedures. As a council member said, "One way to deal with it [the representativeness problem] is to say, 'Well, you set up a structure, there's an open process.' If there's an open process, I don't ask the second question" (p. 98). A Community Development administrator concurred:

"The issue always comes up of, how can you take the word of this group that meets on Thursday nights and assume that they speak for the community? I do think that we have to insist that they have some kind of democratically open procedures. If you can maintain the awareness of people that this group exists, it is going to meet and make recommendations to City Hall . . . then I have no problem whether there's a dozen people or two hundred" (p. 98).

Finally, these administrators also tested the representativeness of community groups by seeking information from others in the city's communities. As one administrator reported, "On any important issue we'll try to contact as many people as possible in addition to the community councils" (p. 98).

After observing and asking questions, most of Cincinnati's administrators claimed that they eventually formed a good reading on the representativeness of particular groups. According to one administrator, "After a while we know who they represent. They may not represent who they say they represent, but we know who they do represent" (p. 98).

Several techniques emerge from the Cincinnati experience as potentially useful for public managers who are attempting to assess the legitimacy of groups they work with. These include:

1. *Membership lists.* How many members can a group document?
2. *Attendance at public hearings.* How many people in attendance identify with the group?
3. *Repeated observations.* To what extent can the group sustain membership and attendance?
4. *Democratic procedures.* Are the group's meetings and decision-making procedures open and democratic?
5. *Multiple sources.* What do others in the community think about community opinion and the representativeness of this group?

To this list might be added other techniques for use with other kinds of groups, such as:

6. *Letters.* Assuming a file of letters from citizens is kept, what do they suggest about public opinion?

7. *Phone complaints and comments.* If a log of phone calls can be maintained, what does it suggest about the division of opinion in the public?

8. *Survey results.* Where a survey has been run, what do the results suggest about the division of opinion in the relevant public?

Seldom, if ever, will any one technique provide information adequate to judge either the legitimacy of particular groups or the nature of broader public opinion. In the end, following the example of Cincinnati's administrators, the public manager is best advised to attempt triangulation, to put together information drawn from a variety of sources to assess who represents whom.

The Role of Other Governmental Actors

The public cannot be considered in isolation from other stakeholders. Before deciding how to involve the public, the manager should consider what other actors, governmental actors in particular, may have a stake sufficient to require their involvement, too. Those actors could include (a) other departments in the same governmental unit, (b) other units of the same governmental level, or (c) other levels of government.

It may now be more important than ever before to involve other governmental actors in resolving many issues. For one thing, many contemporary problems cross traditional functional departmental divisions. Problems such as drug abuse and unemployment often cannot be adequately addressed by a single governmental department, but instead require the cooperative action of many departments and citizens. Similarly, many contemporary problems also cross the boundaries of multiple government bodies. The issues of air pollution and water pollution, as two examples, usually extend across many jurisdictions in the typically fragmented governmental arrangements of American metropolises. Finally, since the expansion of federal grants in the 1960s and early 1970s, many programs involve multiple levels of government.

When an issue arises, the public manager should consider which governmental actors, if any, to involve in deliberations. Excluding important governmental actors could preclude the cooperation essential to implementing an eventual decision. Governmental actors are no less likely than other actors to balk at decisions in which they had no chance to participate, as planners in Corpus Christi, Texas, learned (see Case 4.3, adapted from McClendon and Lewis, 1985).

Case 4.3

Community Goal Setting in Corpus Christi

At the instigation of community leaders, Corpus Christi in 1973 launched "Goals for Corpus Christi," a program designed to define long-term goals for the city. The program "revolved around the following: What are the basic questions the community must resolve to progress? What are the possible answers? What are the pros and cons and background information relevant to considering each answer?" (McClendon and Lewis, 1985, p. 73). The program was also designed to reflect broad public involvement in order to learn "what answers" would "reflect the value system of Corpus Christians." The program's creators recognized that broad public involvement was a prerequisite to successful implementation, what program planners termed "the important implementation consideration" of any goals (p. 77).

Accordingly, city planners structured a process of extensive public involvement designed to give decisions on the goals to city residents. First, a representative fourteen-person steering committee was formed to oversee the entire process. That committee then selected a larger committee "of approximately 100 persons representing a cross-section of the ethnic, sex, age, socioeconomic and leadership composition of the population," a committee that in turn was divided into subcommittees for different goal areas (p. 74). As discussions progressed, subcommittee members visited other community groups to publicize the evolving goals. Finally, a community vote on various goals was solicited through mail-in ballots published in the city's newspapers. To increase interest in voting, on the day of the vote local television stations broadcast video documentaries on the various goal areas. Citizens responded positively: "The effort aroused the interest of thousands of citizens and strengthened the ties between citizens, experts and decision makers. The climate for future community involvement was improved. And at the completion of the goals program more than 10,000 ballot responses had been received" (p. 79).

Still, the resulting goals proved less valuable than had been hoped, producing few successful policy or program initiatives. Unfortunately, the considerable effort to stimulate public involvement was not parallelled by a comparable effort to gain the commitment of municipal administrators. As a consequence, once the program ended, "most public decision makers reverted to the old ways of doing business, and the results were soon forgotten. Some decision makers are not interested in sharing their authority and they will not voluntarily use the results of a Goals program" (p. 79). Much of the value of the extensive public involvement was wasted because municipal administrators were not similarly involved.

———•———

The need to involve other governmental actors often can be accommodated by forming an advisory committee representing all of the interested parties. Corpus Christi had such a mechanism in place, and might easily have avoided the resistance of administrators by including them on the one-hundred-person committee.

The urge to broaden involvement must recognize limits since casting the net too broadly can unnecessarily complicate decision making. Participation should be limited to those who need to be involved, that is, to those who can provide important information or assist in implementation.

The risk of involving too many levels of government may be especially acute. Additional levels of government appear to complicate issues in a manner that has a unique potential for threatening decision effectiveness. The reanalysis of public involvement cases (see also Chapter Five) indicated that, other things being equal, involving more levels of government reduced decision effectiveness. Simply having more actors involved in making the decision did not impair effectiveness.

This is not to suggest that other levels of government with a legitimate interest in an issue should be excluded from decision making. Such exclusion would risk the same kinds of problems Corpus Christi experienced by excluding municipal administrators. Many issues can, however, appropriately be limited to the level of government at which they originated.

Chapter Five

Sharing Decision-Making Authority with the Public

Many issues require that the public manager make decisions with the public. This strategy becomes desirable whenever successful implementation requires public acceptance that cannot be assumed without public involvement. The manager must then choose how this extensive public involvement should be pursued. This chapter examines how to make this choice with the aid of the Effective Decision Model. After presenting the full model, the first part of the chapter explains when to use each of the several advanced approaches to public involvement described in the model. The second part of the chapter then examines possible barriers to taking these approaches, as well as how to overcome the barriers.

The Complete Effective Decision Model

Figure 5.1 summarizes the Effective Decision Model by adding the questions defined in the last chapter to the first steps outlined in Figure 3.1. Tracing answers to the various questions through the model's decision tree will produce a recommendation of which of the five approaches to take toward public involvement on any given issue. In general, concerns for quality recommend less involvement and concerns for acceptability recommend more, but the choice cannot be reduced to a simple additive rule.

The model is designed to aid managers in balancing the competing concerns for legitimacy and effectiveness that arise with public involvement. Use of the model promises to improve the legitimacy of decisions by inviting more public involvement than

Figure 5.1. The Effective Decision Model of Public Involvement.

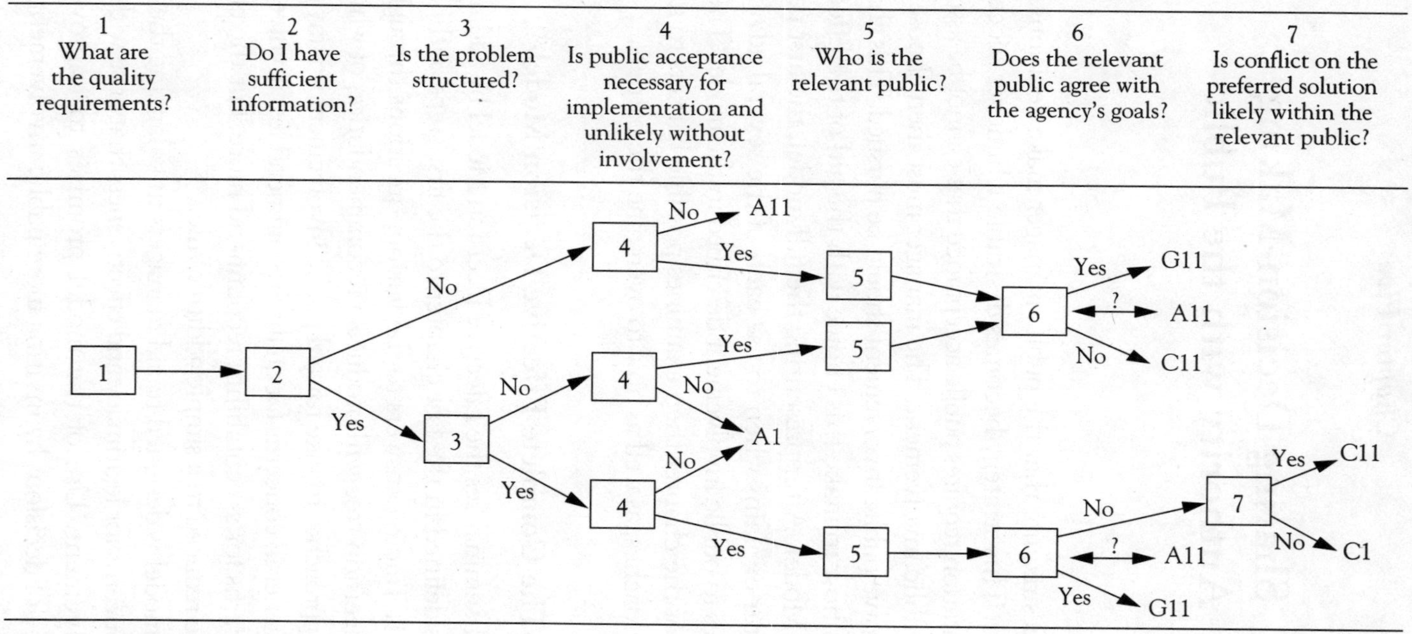

1	2	3	4	5	6	7
What are the quality requirements?	Do I have sufficient information?	Is the problem structured?	Is public acceptance necessary for implementation and unlikely without involvement?	Who is the relevant public?	Does the relevant public agree with the agency's goals?	Is conflict on the preferred solution likely within the relevant public?

Key: A1 = Autonomous managerial decision
A11 = Modified autonomous managerial decision
C1 = Segmented public consultation
C11 = Unitary public consultation
G11 = Public decision

public managers might otherwise invite. Following the model's recommendations can explain much of the variation in the effectiveness of actual governmental decisions in which the public was—or in some cases, was not—involved (see Appendix A for actual research findings).

To use the model to advantage, managers must avoid rigid application of its implied sequence. That is, when an issue arises, the manager should attempt to answer the questions in the model, but should also view the answers as tentative, subject to change. Subsequent developments, often during public involvement, may point to a need to reconsider answers. Feedback from the public could call particular quality requirements into question, as happened to Forest Service staffers in negotiating with public interest groups (see Chapter Three); or mobilization of previously unorganized citizens could reveal that public attitudes differ markedly from what the manager had at first surmised. These or other factors frequently justify reconsidering the nature of issues and, ultimately, the recommendations of the model.

The Effective Decision Model provides only some of the tools public managers need for public involvement. Managers must also be able to choose the right mechanism or form of public involvement, the subject of Chapters Six and Seven.

Three Approaches to Deciding with the Public

Many issues that confront public managers call for extensive public involvement in which influence must be shared with the public. According to the Effective Decision Model, that kind of public involvement should have been invited on 91 percent of the cases studied in the reanalysis described in Chapter Three and Appendix A. These were the cases that included a need for public acceptance that could not be assumed without involvement. The manager can choose from three general approaches to such involvement: the public decision approach, the unitary consultation approach, and the segmented consultation approach. The choice should rest on how the relevant public is thought to feel about the issue, as defined by questions six and seven in the model.

Using the Public Decision Approach

The choice of approach should hinge initially on the anticipated citizen attitudes toward organizational goals, determined by asking the sixth question in the model. If citizens are expected to agree with the agency's goals, the Effective Decision Model recommends maximum public involvement (see the far upper right and lower right parts of the model). Because so little risk to quality is combined with a need for acceptance, the manager should use the public decision approach: deciding jointly with the public.

This recommendation holds regardless of the issue's other characteristics. Information needs and problem structure, in particular, become irrelevant whenever acceptance requiring involvement is needed and the public agrees with agency goals. The need for citizen acceptance that cannot be assumed without involvement calls for extensive public involvement, and the citizen agreement with agency goals indicates that the manager need not worry about quality being compromised in that involvement.

Taking the public decision approach does not mean that the manager surrenders all authority to the public. To the contrary, at the outset of any involvement process the manager must set constraints on the public's authority that reflect the agency's quality requirements as well as any necessary problem structure. Needless to say, the manager should also plan to participate actively in decision-making discussions.

Under the appropriate conditions, the public decision approach can work extremely well. Highly effective decisions are attainable when the public both agrees with agency goals and, by virtue of being involved in decision making, supports the eventual decision. The success of an Oakland, California, tree planting program, described in Case 5.1 (adapted from Sklar and Ames, 1985), is illustrative.

———•———

Case 5.1

Street-Tree Survival in the Inner City

Urban forestry is a relatively new field, dating only to the mid 1960s. Whereas trees in cities have traditionally been viewed as "normal, expected, and taken for granted," a new breed of urban foresters sees trees serving "social, economic, environmental, and public health functions, making them not only expressive objects, but instrumental objects that concretely can influence the quality of city life" (Sklar and Ames, 1985, p. 55).

At the same time, urban foresters also see trees, especially those in the city, as fragile objects. Since most preexisting trees were destroyed in the building of cities, "most urban trees are not native to the area in which they are planted but rather are imported." As a consequence, "trees in an urban setting survive through human action" (p. 56).

Operating from this philosophy and with the aid of public funding, in 1978 urban foresters in Oakland, California, initiated a tree planting program designed to help in revitalizing deteriorated areas of the inner city. Under the rubric of the Oakland Neighborhood Tree Organizing Program, a small paid technical staff and a larger group of volunteers began working with low-income neighborhoods to plant and care for new trees.

The principal quality requirement was a high rate of tree survival. In addition to what they knew in theory about the fragility of urban trees, Oakland's urban foresters could see evidence of fragility in the failure of an earlier Model Cities tree-planting program; as planning for the new program began, only ten trees still stood from the Model Cities planting of two thousand trees less than a decade earlier. There was no need for additional information and no problem structure, but citizen acceptance was essential: "Trees in urban settings survive through human action" to water, feed, prune, and protect (pp. 56–57). In addition, as the failure of the Model Cities program demonstrated, this acceptance could not be assumed without citizen participation given "the historic disinclination of inner-city residents to care for and protect trees" (p. 59). As a final issue characteristic, although this acceptance could not be assumed, citizens could be expected to agree with the noncontroversial goal of tree survival.

The Effective Decision Model recommends the public decision approach for any issue with these characteristics. The need for citizen acceptance demands extensive involvement, and citizen agreement with program goals frees the manager from having to constrain that involvement with anything other than quality requirements. Consistent with this recommendation, program staff in 1977 to 1978 attempted a public decision through a series of neighborhood meetings structured to reach consensus on which trees to plant and where to plant them (p. 59).

The results were predictably positive. The extensive involvement won the necessary acceptance: "Residents participated so intensively in the selection of the trees that they came to believe the trees and parkways were theirs" (p. 63). That acceptance in turn produced an effective outcome: "From the viewpoint of tree survival, the Oakland urban forestry program has been a success . . . largely due to the actions of residents." Of the trees planted, fully "60 to 70 percent . . . were still standing" as of mid 1983, a dramatic improvement from the few which had survived the earlier program (pp. 59–60).

Using the Unitary Consultation Approach

Planning for public involvement becomes more difficult when, in any situation with a need for public acceptance that cannot be assumed without involvement, the manager believes that the public—or some significant segment of the public—does *not* share the agency's goals. The manager now faces competing needs for involvement as a means to obtain public acceptance and for limits on that involvement in order to preserve agency goals.

Issues with these characteristics probably arise frequently. The cases in the reanalysis, though not necessarily representative of all public management decisions, are suggestive on this point. More than 60 percent of those cases found the public disagreeing with agency goals where a need for acceptance required public involvement.

These issues are inherently difficult to resolve to everyone's satisfaction. The differing preferences of the agency and the public often cannot be accommodated by any process of public involvement or by any decision. Looking again at the case reanalysis, almost two thirds of the cases with these characteristics ended in ineffective decisions.

Those decisions might not have proved so ineffective had public managers chosen better approaches to decision making. Although according to the model these issues call for some form of consultation with the public, the public managers responsible for these decisions in the case reanalysis often acted autonomously, with the public permitted at most to provide information. Confronted with difficult issues, these managers may have instinctively preferred the seeming simplicity of a unilateral decision to the inevitably messy process of deciding with the public. Unfortunately, that simplicity can prove short-lived if a dissatisfied public resists imposition of a managerial decision, creating an even messier, perhaps unresolvable impasse.

A better approach to resolving most problems of this nature is the unitary consultation, in which the manager meets with the public as a single group before making a decision. In contrast to the public decision approach, the manager in this case makes the decision away from the public, thereby retaining more authority to incorporate the agency's preferences into the decision. At the same time, both to respect the public's role and to obtain its acceptance, the decision must to some extent reflect the public's preferences.

Managers should employ a unitary consultation first for any issue that features (a) a need for information, (b) no problem structure, (c) a need for acceptance that requires involvement, and (d) public disagreement with the agency's goals (as determined by question six in the top part of the model). The latitude for public influence is so great in a situation in which information is needed and the problem is unstructured that a unitary consultation is recommended despite the public's disagreement with agency goals. Using a unitary consultation, a manager can decide in a manner that reflects both public input and agency priorities.

If the problem were structured, a unitary consultation might still be appropriate. Since structure reduces the latitude for public influence, the manager must consider possible conflict *within* the public, the seventh question in the Effective Decision Model, before deciding how to proceed. If conflict appears likely, a unitary consultation should be employed (as shown in the far right part of the model).

The principal advantage of a unitary consultation in this situation is that it should reveal to a divided public the nature of its divisions. With the full public having the opportunity to speak, those divisions should quickly become evident to everyone in attendance. Increased awareness of the divisions may then enhance the public's understanding of the difficulty the manager faces in trying to shape a decision that bridges those differences. Such understanding should in turn increase the likelihood of public acceptance of the eventual decision.

This is another situation in which the recommended approach runs counter to the instincts of many public managers and policy makers. Faced with a divided public, managers may prefer approaches that suppress rather than facilitate the voicing of conflict. The danger is that those alternative approaches may produce less effective decisions, as illustrated by the Bellingham, Washington, economic development initiative profiled in Case 5.2 (adapted from Fox, 1985).

Case 5.2

Defeating a Bond Referendum in a Declining City, Part I

Located about midway between Seattle, Washington, and Vancouver, British Columbia, Bellingham is a city of approximately forty-eight thousand people. In the late 1970s when this issue arose, the city's downtown was aging, with some buildings dating to the nineteenth century. Although still "prosperous," the downtown lacked "space for the major stores to expand and provide convenient parking" (Fox, 1985, p. 29).

Civic leaders became concerned for the future of the downtown when a local developer announced plans in 1979 to build a large shopping mall on the outskirts of the city. "This mall was widely perceived as a threat to the vitality of the city core and identity of the whole community." Civic leaders saw a need to revitalize the downtown so that "it would remain the major shopping center for the region." To assist in that effort, the Downtown Development Task Force was appointed and charged with "modernizing" the downtown and "retaining and adding major retailers" (p. 29).

With the encouragement of the task force, a Canadian development firm eventually put forth a proposal to build a competing mall in the downtown. The firm offered to invest $48 million in private money if the city would spend $16 million on utility improvements and build two new parking garages.

The city council liked the proposal, but needed a way to pay for the parking facilities. To avoid tax increases, "the city decided to pay for the two parking garages with revenue that the project itself would generate." The city proposed to raise approximately $7 million from general obligation bonds, which would be paid off with the increased tax revenues anticipated from the mall. There was some risk to the city, however, because "money from the general fund would have to be used to retire the bonds if the development failed to increase revenue" (p. 30). For that and other reasons, opponents challenged the plan, and gained enough signatures in a petition drive to force a referendum on whether the city could issue the bonds.

Stated in terms of the Effective Decision Model, this problem featured as its principal quality requirement—in the eyes of the Bellingham city officials and civic leaders—to redevelop the downtown to an extent sufficient to repel the threat of the proposed suburban mall; but the city clearly lacked information on citizen preferences (p. 38). With the forcing of the referendum, the problem also acquired the structure of a no-longer-negotiable "yes-no" choice. In addition, the referendum meant by definition that (a) citizen acceptance was necessary for successful implementation, (b) acceptance could not be assumed without involvement, and (c) many citizens did not share the city's redevelopment goals.

At the same time, as a final problem attribute, citizens disagreed among themselves, with only a minority opposing the whole idea of a large shopping center in the downtown. Many opposed only "the spending of public revenue in conjunction with a private investment activity" (pp. 35–36).

This is the sort of issue for which the Effective Decision Model favors a unitary consultation, soliciting ideas from the full public, such as through public hearings or meetings with a representative advisory committee, in part to raise awareness of the differences within the public. In the Bellingham case, that approach might have built support for the city's dilemma in trying to formulate a decision satisfactory to everyone.

The city instead pursued an autonomous or modified autonomous approach, appointing a citizen advisory committee that proved to be neither representative, "consist(ing) mostly of sympathetic citizens from the middle of the ideological spectrum," nor influential in formulating the development plan (p. 38). City officials retained full authority over the decision, using the committee only as a source of information, if that.

That departure from the recommended approach helps to explain why voters rejected the city's plans, approving the referendum proposal by a 52 to 48 percent margin in November 1982. The city's failure to consult at once with all of the various public factions helped to turn voters against the city's plan. In a city plagued by recession and hungry for economic development, the lack of appropriate public involvement killed a proposal that might have brought significant economic development (p. 36).

Using the Segmented Consultation Approach

Perhaps the most difficult situation finds the manager needing public acceptance on a structured issue in which, as shown in the far lower right part of the model, citizens are opposed to organizational goals as well as united among themselves in that opposition. The manager must somehow reach agreement with a public that opposes what the agency hoped to achieve on an issue in which little latitude is available for public influence. The public must be extensively involved, but that involvement must be circumscribed in order to respect the agency's quality requirements and the structure of the problem.

The best means to achieve those competing ends may be to consult separately with different segments of the public, avoiding meeting with the full public as a whole. Consistent with that logic, the Effective Decision Model recommends a segmented consultation for dealing with such issues. The value of this approach is suggested by Mario Cuomo's classic mediation of a New York City housing dispute, as described in Case 5.3 (adapted from Gillers, 1980).

———•———

Case 5.3

Mediating the Forest Hills
Housing Dispute, Part I

Public housing for low-income families ranks high on the list of most disliked "LULUs" among middle-income neighborhoods. The dislike can be especially acute when racial differences overlap the income differences, sometimes resulting in middle-income whites feeling that their neighborhoods are being "invaded" by low-income minorities (Gillers, 1980, p. 62). It should have been no surprise then when residents of the almost exclusively white and middle-income Forest Hills area of New York City objected in 1971 to the construction in their neighborhood of 840 apartments for low-income, mostly minority families.

The proposal for the housing had been under discussion for at least five years, but no action had been taken. The city meanwhile was gradually moving toward construction without any sense of the likely reaction in the neighborhood. The objections of Forest Hills residents were all the more strident because the construction caught them by surprise, the five years of inaction having created a "sense of security" in the neighborhood that the housing would never be built. When residents suddenly saw the construction underway, "almost as fast as a fire spreads through an old wooden building, the community became polarized. Residents organized into opposition groups. Pickets appeared. Violence was threatened and city officials took the threats seriously. National attention focused on Forest Hills" (p. 65).

Mario Cuomo, then a Queens lawyer, was asked to assist after the neighborhood reaction halted the housing construction. In addition to quality requirements imposed by the federal government (including a maximum allowable construction cost per housing unit and a scatter-site requirement to place the housing in a middle-income area), the problem Cuomo faced was structured: since construction had already begun, choice was limited to how many units would be constructed. A need for information on citizen preferences was evident in Cuomo's choice of "fact gathering as his primary task" (p. 70). Citizen acceptance obviously was essential for implementation and could not be assumed without participation. Finally, the most vexing part of the problem was that neighborhood residents appeared to be united in their opposition.

Cuomo chose to approach the issue through a segmented consultation, soliciting ideas separately from each of a number of citizen groups and their representatives. He apparently recognized the several principles underlying the appropriateness of this approach for the dispute: an acute need for acceptance required significant public participation, but citizen antipathy to quality requirements ruled out a public decision and problem structure and the united public opposition ruled out a unitary consultation.

The consistency of Cuomo's strategy with the model's recommendation helps to explain why his decision proved relatively successful: the stalemate was broken, residents accepted the project, and "the project was built substantially as Cuomo recommended" (p. 83). The outcome was not entirely satisfactory—costs to the city rose, and only half of the original construction goal was achieved—but such highly conflictual problems seldom can be resolved to everyone's satisfaction.

As the Forest Hills case illustrates, taking the appropriate approach to issues that call for a unitary consultation does not guarantee a successful outcome. These kinds of problems (another example would be the siting of a hazardous waste disposal facility) are inherently difficult to resolve satisfactorily. Public acceptance is essential for implementation, and involvement is necessary to obtain that acceptance, but the public does not share the agency's goals (although the public may be divided in this opposition).

If the public is not involved appropriately in an issue of this kind, successful resolution becomes even less likely. Whatever its flaws, the compromise Cuomo achieved in the Forest Hills dispute was superior to the impasse and open conflict that preceded his intervention.

Using Multiple Approaches

With many issues, public managers should employ more than one approach to public involvement. The complexity of the issue, the complexity of the relevant public, or some other factor often calls for using a combination of decision-making approaches.

A combination of approaches may be desirable, for example, when the manager begins with little information about public preferences. That lack of information could call for an initial limited public involvement as a means for learning about public preferences, followed by a more extensive involvement once some knowledge of those preferences is gained. Such a strategy might have produced a different outcome to the Bellingham downtown renewal issue, as further explored in Case 5.4 (adapted from Fox, 1985).

Case 5.4

Defeating a Bond Referendum in a Declining City, Part II

Had the Effective Decision Model been employed in the Bellingham case, the city's civic and political leaders might have quickly realized that they lacked answers to important questions about the nature of public preferences. According to Fox, these leaders lacked information "about the preferences of opponents," in part because many of the opponents were "at the outset . . . unorganized and splintered into many different factions" (p. 38).

The city's leaders proceeded nonetheless to appoint a citizens advisory committee. Not surprisingly, given the lack of knowledge of public preferences, that committee proved unrepresentative: "It failed to provide a forum for the more alienated segments from the ideological poles who opposed the project" (p. 38). The eventual defeat of the bond referendum traces in part to that unrepresentativeness.

A better choice for the city might have been to seek information on public preferences before appointing any committee. Fox (p. 38) in fact recommended that the city could have surveyed residents to learn their preferences. In so doing, the city would have utilized the modified autonomous managerial decision-making approach, attempting to gain information from the public without any promise of influence for the public.

With completion of the survey, the city should have known enough about public preferences to recognize the need for a second decision-making approach with more extensive public involvement. Since the divisions within the public indicated the need for a unitary consultation, consulting with the public as a whole, public involvement could have been pursued through an advisory committee more representative of the public, public hearings designed to attract unorganized publics, or a combination of both.

Such a two-part approach would have been much more likely to produce an outcome satisfactory to the city's leaders. The city might have needed to revise its bond proposal to accommodate public opinion and win public support, but that revised proposal might then have been approved, giving the city a partial victory instead of a total loss.

A combination of decision-making approaches is also often desirable when advisory committees are used. Since an advisory committee is unlikely to articulate public opinion perfectly, the manager may want to employ public hearings as a check on the committee. If, as seems likely, the manager does not want to give equal authority to both the committee and the hearings, the public might only be consulted, with a public decision approach taken by the committee. The two approaches in tandem give principal authority to the committee, yet also provide an opportunity for direct expression of public opinion.

Overcoming Barriers to Public Involvement

Can managers always involve the public as extensively as may seem desirable? In practice, other demands on the decision-making process—in particular, regulatory requirements or a time constraint—could pose barriers to following the Effective Decision Model's recommendations for such extensive involvement. Anecdotal reports suggest that public managers often see these demands as competing with the need for public involvement.

This argument does not stand up well under close scrutiny. Closer examination reveals, for one thing, that barriers to public involvement are less imposing than they at first appear. In addition, far from being helpless in the face of constraints, managers are often able to avoid potential barriers by acting *before* they can be erected. Both points warrant elaboration.

In regard to the severity of the constraints, consider first the supposed burden of legislative and regulatory requirements. In the cases examined in the reanalysis, these requirements seldom stipulated the extent and form of public involvement. Instead, in almost every case public managers were left with either some choice or broad choice about how to involve the public (see also Chapter Three and Appendix A).

Interestingly, having broader choice does not necessarily result in a better choice. Decision makers in the reanalysis who had that broad choice selected a level of involvement consistent with the Effective Decision Model in only 36 percent of the cases. By contrast, decision makers limited to some choice selected the appropriate level of involvement in 58 percent of the cases. Rather than hindering public involvement, regulatory requirements have worked—historically at least—in a salutary manner to persuade decision makers to involve the public in a manner more appropriate to the issues at hand. These requirements may have forced managers to abandon their traditional reflexive tendency to exclude the public from deliberations on difficult issues.

Consider next the possibility that a time constraint may force the public manager to limit public involvement. This idea has strong theoretical roots that can be traced to the original theory on which the Effective Decision Model is based. According to Vroom and Yetton (1973), a time constraint may call for less involvement than would otherwise appear desirable, without threatening eventual decision effectiveness.

More recently, however, these theorists have recanted that argument. In an analysis of time constraints reported by private sector managers, Vroom and Jago (1988, p. 87) found that "most of these managers are citing a severe time constraint simply to justify or rationalize their preferred autocratic style. When so-called crises are examined, we find that there was almost always ample time to undo a bad decision although a pressure of time was cited as the reason for the poor decision in the first place." For these managers, a time constraint was more often an inappropriate excuse than a legitimate reason for limiting involvement.

Findings from the case reanalysis suggest similarly that a time constraint by itself cannot justify limiting public involvement. First, the reanalysis provided no evidence in favor of less public involvement in effective decisions made under time pressures than in effective decisions made without those pressures. Nor was there evidence that time constraints reduced the likelihood of an effective decision. Time constraints did not appear to affect how the public should be involved in resolving such issues.

This apparent unimportance of a time constraint can be explained by examining how time actually constrains public managers. First, time constraints on the making of public decisions often prove more flexible than they appear, especially if an aroused public resists a quick decision. The manager who then reduces public involvement to save time risks increased public opposition, endangering rather than facilitating an effective decision. Second, public managers face time constraints on implementation as well as on decision making, and the two constraints are inversely related. Time spent to involve more actors in decision making can expedite implementation by winning the support of those who are involved. Conversely, time saved by excluding actors from decision making can slow implementation because those who were excluded may resist and delay that process.

Public managers should consequently be cautious about seeing a time constraint as grounds for limiting public involvement. A manager who perceives a time constraint should first question its necessity. If the constraint appears valid, the manager should then weigh time constraints on *both* decision making and implementation. In the end, whenever possible, the manager is best advised to ignore time constraints in deciding how to involve the public.

The other aspect of overcoming barriers to public involvement is for public managers to try to take action *before* barriers can be erected. To repeat the advice offered in Chapter Three, public managers should initiate issues rather than let issues be forced upon them. Initiating action gives managers more ability to guide the development of issues, increasing the likelihood that a decision can be reached before time pressures can become an issue.

Initiating early action also facilitates defining issues in terms more amenable to solutions satisfactory to all sides. Agency priorities can be protected by the early assertion of terms, and public involvement can be invited before an issue becomes rigidly defined, as in the Forest Hills case, in a manner that circumscribes potential public influence.

Following this advice should not mean that the manager in any way preempts the articulation of real public concerns. Initiating action before the sides on an issue become polarized and before external constraints are imposed should actually facilitate full expression of all shades of public opinion, as well as of agency and managerial priorities.

Earlier initiation of issues is easier to achieve, too, if the manager pursues public involvement aggressively, treating that involvement as integral to the managerial process. When involvement is integral and ongoing, the manager can learn about public preferences and concerns as they develop, and thereby initiate discussion of emerging issues more readily, before they become intractable crises.

Chapter Six

Involving the Public for Information Only

After determining how much the public should be involved, the public manager must select techniques by which to pursue that involvement. Three decades of experimentation have generated a wide range of choices that continues to grow with advances in communications technology. In general, the options can be dichotomized into techniques designed (1) only to obtain information or (2) to obtain public acceptance while offering influence in exchange. This chapter examines the first type.

Techniques targeted only at obtaining information must respect two principles. First, since influence may not be given in exchange for the information, the techniques must demand minimal time and effort on the part of citizens who become involved—for instance, the five or ten minutes that may be required for a citizen to answer a few questions about city services in a phone survey. Many people will volunteer that much time without expecting influence in return. Second, these techniques should involve citizens as individuals rather than assembling them as a group. In addition to violating the first principle by requiring that citizens take the time and make the effort to gather, assembling citizens as a group increases the potential of their mobilizing and demanding influence.

The techniques that meet these two criteria include (1) key contacts, (2) citizen-initiated contacts with agencies, (3) citizen surveys, and (4) new communications technologies. The remainder of this chapter considers each of those techniques in turn, including how they work, the advantages and disadvantages they may bring, and when each should be used.

Key Contacts

The most rudimentary form of public involvement is when a manager consults with "key contacts" in the relevant public (Hendee and others, 1976, p. 135). This approach entails asking a small number of individuals, usually leaders of organized groups, to comment on particular issues.

Advantages and Disadvantages

A number of problems are associated with consulting key contacts as a form of public involvement. Most obviously, it is difficult to identify the few individuals who can speak authoritatively for any larger public; the manager may have no immediate means for judging who particular individuals actually speak for. The best test of the wisdom of key contacts may come through eventual public reaction to a decision, but by then it is probably too late to change the decision if the contacts prove to have been out of touch with public opinion. In addition, key contacts who prove to be good sources of information on one issue cannot be assumed to be good sources on other issues. A previously dormant public with a very different perspective might have coalesced without the key contacts' awareness; a difference between the old issue and the new could prompt a public response different from what contacts anticipate; or these contacts may simply have lost touch with the public. These problems have given the consulting of key contacts a poor reputation as a form of public involvement. For many advocates of public involvement, the use of key contacts smacks of traditional undemocratic practices in which managers listen to the opinions of a few elites, ignoring the views of the larger public.

Nevertheless, consulting key contacts should not be abandoned as a contemporary approach to public involvement. Used appropriately, this approach has important advantages. For one thing, the lack of formal structure permits the generation of high-quality information: "Input can be obtained in person, one-on-one, in depth, and in detail" (Hendee and others, 1976, p. 135). Second, the use of key contacts requires little formal planning or expertise. If contacts can be identified, the manager can informally call or visit, rather than having to plan carefully for meetings of larger publics. Third, consulting with key contacts ordinarily requires little or no sharing of decision-making authority. The contributions asked of the contacts, such as opinions expressed in brief phone conversations, is usually so modest that no influence is anticipated in return.

When to Use This Technigue

The advantages of this technique outweigh the disadvantages only if the manager is careful about when and how key contacts are used. First, key contacts are rarely appropriate resources for learning the opinions of an unorganized public. The lack of organization ordinarily means that this public has not selected leaders. The manager who relies on key contacts for information about this public in effect assumes the risky job of guessing who those leaders might be if the public were to organize.

A common error of public managers and policy makers in the use of key contacts is to assume that leaders of organized groups can also speak for the unorganized. In the Port Townsend terminal siting case profiled in Chapter Four, for example, the Washington State planners made the mistake of assuming that the town's traditional leaders could identify who should be represented on an advisory committee. When those key contacts overlooked the town's unorganized newcomers, the advisory committee lost legitimacy. The committee could not speak for all major interests in the community, and its initial decision could not be implemented.

By contrast, the use of key contacts can be both appropriate and necessary when the relevant public is comprised principally of one or more organized groups. The official leaders of those groups are obvious nominees as key contacts. In fact, the manager who does not consult with those leaders, assuming public involvement is needed, may appear to challenge the legitimacy of the groups.

The optimal use of key contacts in public involvement requires, however, that the manager not settle for the obvious nominees. To avoid the technique's representational weaknesses, the manager should seek additional nominations and try to talk with those additional people. Such an aggressive approach can result in consultation with key contacts being a representative and effective form of public involvement, as illustrated by Mario Cuomo's approach to mediating the Forest Hills Housing dispute, begun in Case 5.3 and continued in Case 6.1 (adapted from Gillers, 1980).

Case 6.1

Mediating the Forest Hills
Housing Dispute, Part II

Key contacts did not initially figure prominently in Mario Cuomo's approach to the dispute over the building of public housing in Forest Hills. Instead, believing that the "community must be given an opportunity to express itself," Cuomo began by listening to "anyone who wanted to come" to his office (Gillers, 1980, p. 71).

This proved a time-consuming process, however, and Cuomo had given himself only six weeks to resolve the issue. Consequently, he changed strategies after a month, deciding he would now only "be able to see 'leaders,'" key contacts who spoke for important interests in the community (p. 71).

Cuomo decided at the same time to move more actively toward resolving the issue. Having listened to all comers for that first month, Cuomo chose now "to take various actions in order to more rapidly crystallize the issues and learn if, indeed, there was any middle area within which both sides might compromise" (p. 71). He began to play a "devil's advocate" role, challenging the adamant opposition many community leaders had voiced to low-income housing.

This approach helped to create a "psychology of compromise" by which these community leaders, the key contacts, saw the need to give ground. "Cuomo then began informally to suggest various actual compromises, to be tested by word of mouth in the community" (p. 73). This approach culminated, of course, in a compromise accepted, if not embraced, by all sides.

Key contacts proved effective in this case for several reasons. First, by virtue of his initial "open door" approach, Cuomo gained a feel for who the key contacts might be. Instead of following any predetermined enumeration of key contacts, Cuomo used the initial fact-finding process to identify key contacts specific to the issue.

Second, rather than stopping there, Cuomo sought out other leaders from whom he was not hearing, such as the supporters of the housing project. Recognizing the risk of accepting the "conclusion that the most vocal are the most representative" (p. 75), Cuomo looked for other, less vocal leaders to ensure that he heard from all sides of the issue.

Third, consulting key contacts was not the only form of public involvement employed. At the front end of the process, Cuomo listened to anyone from the public who wanted to talk about the issue. At the back end, he relied upon key contacts to catalyze word-of-mouth testing of proposed solutions among the broader public. All of this was also part of a mediation approach to public involvement (see Chapter Seven). In other words, one reason the use of key contacts was effective was that it was combined with other techniques that permitted broader public involvement.

Cuomo's success demonstrates that consulting key contacts can be an effective approach to public involvement, and an approach that can provide more than information. The effectiveness rests, however, on using the key contacts in a manner that is far different from the traditional limited consultation with a few key community leaders who are known to the manager before an issue arises.

————•————

Consulting with key contacts can be useful at several stages in a decision-making process. The most common use may be as the first step in information gathering, when key contacts can advise managers on the nature of the relevant public and on what other techniques of involvement may be appropriate. However, as the Forest Hills case illustrates, key contacts can also be useful late in decision making when the details of a decision are being negotiated.

Seldom, if ever, should the use of key contacts be the only form of public involvement. Doubts about key contacts are too great for managers to act confidently on the opinions of these few individuals. Consulting key contacts may be most useful as a supplement to other forms of public involvement. When public meetings are held as the principal form of involvement, the manager may also want to consult informally with key contacts on their reactions to ideas generated in those meetings. Use of key contacts can also be incorporated into another involvement technique, as Cuomo recognized. In the rare case in which consulting key contacts is employed as the principal form of public involvement, the manager should almost certainly use other techniques to check the information those contacts provide.

Citizen-Initiated Contacts

Another kind of contact that public managers can look to for information on public preferences is the so-called citizen-initiated contact, in which citizens initiate contact with a government agency to request a service, to lodge a complaint about a service or the agency, or to register some other opinion. Here the citizen is usually seeking a specific response in the very immediate future, such as, in the extreme case, with a call to a fire department to put out a fire.

Citizen contacts appear to have grown dramatically in volume in recent decades, probably as a by-product of the expansion of the administrative side of government in the 1960s and 1970s. Perhaps because they recognize that many important governmental decisions are now made by administrators, citizens have increasingly voiced their concerns about programs and services to those administrators. In contrast to their declining turnout for elections, citizens have exhibited growing interest in contacting governmental agencies about services that affect their daily lives. Survey evidence from a variety of cities, for example, puts the proportion of citizens who contact local government in any given year in the range of 40 to 55 percent, roughly twice the rate of voter turnout for municipal elections (see Vedlitz and Veblen, 1980, p. 33; Thomas, 1982, p. 508).

Citizen-initiated contacts can serve as an important vehicle for public involvement in two ways. Most obviously, they provide a means for individual citizens to become involved and to spur action on their immediate problems with services, such as by getting a fire extinguished or a pothole filled. Many local governments have established "hot lines" or "action offices" to give citizens a single place to call with these concerns. The evidence on the effectiveness of contacts is generally positive, too, with most citizens reporting satisfaction with how public administrators respond (see, for example, Goodsell, 1983; Thomas, 1986).

As a form of public involvement in decision making, citizen contacts can also provide information to alert public officials to problems with agency programs. Citizen contacts have served this function with the federal Surface Mining Control and Reclamation Act. Desai (1989, pp. 58–59) has documented that "citizen complaints have been the most frequent type of participatory mechanism used by individual citizens" in response to this major federal environmental initiative. The complaints have had an effect: "Over one third of the citizen complaints triggered mine inspections, and about 30 percent of such inspections resulted in enforcement action."

Cumulative data on these contacts can furnish additional useful information to managers. With the growth in the frequency of these contacts and the concurrent improvements in data-collection techniques, many governmental agencies have established procedures for tallying and assessing calls of this nature in order to provide such data.

Advantages and Disadvantages

Citizen-initiated contacts offer several advantages as a source of information on public opinion. First, in contrast to key contacts, citizen-initiated contacts reflect the opinions of a larger population, sometimes a very large population, given the volume of these contacts. Second, the manager need not wonder whether these opinions are strongly or weakly held. The very act of initiating a contact indicates that the citizen feels some intensity about the opinion or request being voiced. Third, these data can be relatively inexpensive, assuming their availability through an existing data collection system. (It can be expensive, however, to acquire and implement such a system if it is not already in place.) Fourth, as records of contacts accumulate, they can be used to track how feelings or problems with services may have changed. These trend data can help if, for example, a question is raised about whether a service has deteriorated in quality.

These contacts also have disadvantages. The principal disadvantage of citizen-initiated contacts is that even if they reflect the opinions of many, they may not reflect majority opinions. Judging from the evidence, contacts reflect principally the opinions of service users, especially middle- to higher-income service users (see, for example, Thomas, 1982, p. 517). Consequently, these contacts should be used only cautiously to answer questions about either low-income service consumers or potential consumers. Similarly, while they often provide good information on existing services, these contacts may have little value for assessing public opinion on new services, emerging problems, or larger policy issues. Citizen-initiated contacts provide only a very circumscribed kind of information.

There is also a potential for citizen contacts to be manipulated. Recognizing the sensitivity of congressional representatives to constituent contacts, organized interest groups have developed sophisticated techniques to generate more contacts on specific legislative issues. "The U.S. Chamber of Commerce, for instance, is about to begin a phone bank that will call the chamber's 215,000 members about issues of interest to the organization. Those who answer will be able to press 1 to have a mailgram or letter sent in their name to their representative, press 2 to record a voice-mail message for the lawmaker or press 3 to have a computer connect them immediately with the lawmaker's office" ("Using public rage," 1993). Such approaches cast doubts on the significance of the resulting contacts. So far they have been targeted mostly at elective officials, but public administrators could be targeted in the future, especially if data from contacts are used in making decisions.

When to Use This Technique

Data from citizen-initiated contacts are most useful in assessing intense public opinions about existing services. If a manager is concerned about a possible problem with a service, citizen contacts may be a good source of data on how great a problem agency clients perceive and whether they see the problem as growing or declining. Data from contacts can also be useful for monitoring the pulse of the public. Trends in citizen-initiated contacts can alert managers to emerging problems, perhaps enabling the manager to act before a problem becomes severe. In both cases, citizen-initiated contacts provide the manager with information on public opinion without offering influence in exchange. Citizens who initiate contacts usually hope to influence agency behavior on a one-time basis on the delivery of a specific service. Any use managers may later make of cumulative data on these contacts need not imply more influence.

Conversely, data from these contacts will be of limited or no value when managers assess new programs or services that depart significantly from the traditional. Contacts might then provide no more than a list of possible service users to ask for reactions to proposed innovations.

Citizen Surveys

Managers often need to obtain information from an even more representative public without sharing any of their decision-making authority. Achieving both goals can be difficult because, when they are not compensated financially, citizens may expect influence in exchange for the assistance they give.

The citizen survey represents one of the few options available to the manager under these circumstances. The standard five-to-fifteen minute phone interview asks citizens for only a small amount of time and information, a "donation" most citizens will volunteer without any quid pro quo. In addition, because citizen opinions are aired individually rather than in a group setting, the likelihood is minimized that the mere act of soliciting information could build public sentiment on the issue.

Advantages and Disadvantages

The principal advantage of the citizen survey is the potential of generalizing results to a larger population. Assuming that respondents are randomly selected from the population (such as by lottery, giving everyone in the population an equal chance of selection), the findings from a sample as small as a few hundred citizens may provide findings representative of a city's full population. By contrast, managers can wonder whether the feelings expressed by a few citizens at a public meeting can be generalized at all. As Miller and Miller (1991, p. 8) have argued, "The citizen survey finds and gives voice to all types of citizens, the poorer as well as the better educated residents, those whose health may keep them from attending meetings and those in better health, shy people and outgoing people, newcomers and old-timers, and those who have a dispassionate point of view as well as those who are emotionally involved. The representative sample tapped in a citizen survey provides the point of view that can be found only in the community at large." A small random sample also provides findings more generalizable than those from a much larger nonrandom sample, such as a mail-in survey published in a newspaper, to which thousands of people might respond.

When conducted regularly, surveys can also furnish excellent information on trends in citizen opinions and perceptions. Asking the same questions of citizens at regular intervals may, in fact, be the best means for determining how public opinion changes. For just that reason, many governmental units now conduct surveys on an annual or biannual basis. At the local level, for example, 61.7 percent of municipal governments in cities with a population of more than fifty thousand reported using citizen surveys as early as 1982 (Johnson and Hein, 1983, p. 242).

Surveys are hardly perfect sources of information. For one thing, responses to survey questions are sensitive to slight changes in question wording. As Stipak (1983, p. 252) has noted, "small changes in wording and context might determine whether a question measures reactions to a specific program, or simply general attitudes toward government." In addition, responses to survey questions cannot be assumed to be strong and enduring. Opinions citizens give on low-visibility issues, in particular, may reflect little thought, and so could change markedly if those issues become the subject of public debate. Opinions from a particular survey are consequently best viewed as "snapshots in time" and subject to change (Milbrath,

1981, p. 482). This latter limitation can be overcome by repeating the same survey at regular intervals, transforming that snapshot into a valuable moving picture of trends in public opinion.

Another problem associated with surveys is that the opinions expressed in them may not offer the best indicators of *intensity* of feelings about issues. How strongly a respondent says he or she feels about the issue may reveal less about intensity than might an *action* the individual takes in support of the feeling. The simple act of attending a public hearing, joining in a public protest, or contacting the relevant agency may say much more about intensity than does any survey opinion.

Third, the survey is a relatively inflexible technique. It offers only limited opportunity to learn how opinions might change under various scenarios, such as when parties with stakes in an issue begin to negotiate a solution. As Milbrath (1981, p. 482) has said, the survey is "not an adequate substitute for the dynamic interaction and development of ideas that can occur in face-to-face discussion."

Fourth, for the results to have value, the manager must know that the questionnaire instrument was carefully constructed, the sample randomly drawn, and the actual interviews impartially conducted. Interviews should be attempted in the evening when residents are home, and multiple calls will be necessary to reach many in the sample. All of that takes time, probably months rather than weeks, and time is sometimes at a premium. However, given the findings reported in Chapter Five, a time constraint probably does not constitute sufficient grounds to decide against a survey.

Fifth, the results of surveys must be interpreted cautiously. It can be difficult to know, for example, what level of satisfaction to expect for particular programs or services. Fortunately, the increasing use of surveys over the past quarter century has helped in establishing benchmark data that can be used to aid in interpreting findings on many programs and services. To take just one area, based on an extensive review of municipal citizen surveys, Miller and Miller (1991, pp. 119–133) have formulated guidelines for interpreting survey findings on satisfaction with a variety of municipal services.

Meeting benchmark standards usually requires the hiring of outside consultants at substantial cost. Few organizations have in-house staff with (a) the necessary expertise to construct a survey, (b) prior training on how to conduct surveys, and (c) the evening work schedules necessary to do the calling. Without all of those capabilities, the survey may not provide information that can be trusted. The manager must consequently weigh whether the potential benefits of a survey are worth the costs of outside assistance.

Often the best choice is to undertake the survey cooperatively, using the consultant for special expertise but using in-house staff for much of the actual labor. To conduct its resident surveys, for example, the city of Auburn, Alabama, has collaborated with public administration faculty and students at Auburn University. Faculty and municipal staff shared responsibility for constructing questions, students performed the interviews, and municipal staff coded and processed the data (Watson, Juster, and Johnson, 1991, p. 234). In addition to reducing the expense of hiring consultants, this approach can build staff understanding and ownership, increasing the likelihood of survey results that are useful to the agency. In the Auburn case, researchers found a "strong consensus . . . among elected officials that survey data are valuable to them as they establish priorities for the city budget" (Watson, Juster, and Johnson, 1991, p. 238).

When to Use This Technique

A citizen survey can be a good choice when (a) the manager is uncertain about public opinion on an issue, (b) the options for action on the issue are clearly defined, and (c) there is a complex public of multiple organized and unorganized groups. The first criterion should be obvious, but the latter two warrant brief explanation. A survey can be more useful when the options are clear because questions can then be framed to ask about those options. A survey can work well with a complex public because random selection facilitates reaching all segments of that public. The value of surveys is evident, for example, in the Tennessee recycling initiative profiled in Case 6.2 (adapted from Bacot and others, 1993).

------•------

Case 6.2

Using Citizen Surveys in Designing Recycling Programs

Environmental concerns and decreasing public tolerance for landfills have prompted growing community interest in recycling, but recycling cannot succeed without public support. "A community solid waste recycling program is a premier example of a service whose ultimate success depends heavily upon citizen commitment and willingness to produce it" (Bacot and others, 1993, p. 30).

Citizen surveys can prove to be useful tools in designing such programs. As Bacot and his coauthors explained, "Well-designed and carefully analyzed citizen opinion surveys can facilitate public acceptance and long-term participation in solid waste recycling, especially in those jurisdictions where participation is voluntary" (p. 30).

To facilitate that acceptance in Tennessee, researchers at the Waste Management Research and Education Institute at the University of Tennessee, Knoxville, examined opinions about various recycling options among the state's residents. A random sample of 844 Tennessee adults were polled by phone in early 1989.

The results suggested broad support for a variety of recycling options. Fully 91 percent of the respondents were "willing" or "strongly willing" to separate waste for curbside collection; 87 percent "favored" or "strongly favored" separating recyclable materials by household; and 82 percent "favored" or "strongly favored" a state law to require a recycling program in every county (pp. 33–34).

There were notable differences in respondent support for some options. Support proved broadest for "those options which require minimal behavioral modification." For example, "those persons living in smaller, rural settings, who already take their household waste to a disposal facility, prefer drop boxes" (p. 37).

The survey also revealed an interesting contrast in opinions on the financing of recycling programs. Sixty-nine percent of residents expressed willingness to pay a monthly fee to help cover the costs of a local recycling program, but a 57 percent majority were "against" or "strongly against" reducing the frequency of waste collection service to help cover those costs (p. 34).

These findings could have considerable relevance for officials in Tennessee who must plan recycling programs. Given the generalizability of the survey results, due to the random selection of respondents, officials should see clear program directions implied by respondents' opinions.

The findings could be especially useful because the Tennessee situation fit the three criteria noted earlier. Managers/policy makers were uncertain about public opinion on various recycling options; those options were clear, such that questions could be framed about specific recycling and financing alternatives; and, the relevant public was complex, composed of all consumers. As the study's authors noted, "Environmental activists typically constitute an important base of support for recycling programs, but extensive efforts to involve other groups in program design and implementation are essential" (p. 38). The survey provided a means to that end.

At the same time, illustrative of a common limitation of surveys, the directions suggested by the findings could not necessarily be implemented without further public involvement. Surveys can be an excellent source of information, but they are not designed to obtain the public acceptance and support that successful recycling programs require. In addition, opinions about recycling options could change if those options become the subject of public discussion. The support for a recycling fee, for example, might erode if an antitax citizens group were to voice opposition. This survey could be an excellent first step in public involvement, but probably not the only step.

Surveys are unlikely to be a good choice when the relevant public consists of one or a few organized groups, such as the residents of a particular neighborhood. Assuming that those groups have leaders who purport to speak for their constituents, a manager who proposes to survey those constituents anyway in effect questions the legitimacy of those leaders. The cost of a survey is also difficult to justify if adequate information can be obtained by less-expensive means. The better choice here may be to talk with the leaders, or to meet with the members (for example, at regular group meetings), or both.

As the Tennessee case illustrates, a survey will often be an early step in public involvement, with the results then used in planning additional public involvement. For instance, in the Bellingham, Washington, downtown redevelopment case discussed in Chapter Five, the city might have used a survey as a first step prior to inviting more extensive public involvement, thereby averting, perhaps, the eventual appointment of an unrepresentative advisory committee.

Surveys can become even more useful when repeated at regular intervals. Data are then readily available for use by administrators in assessing trends in citizen evaluations of government, rather than requiring a separate planning process. In addition, since the surveys are conducted anyway, little additional cost is required to obtain the information.

New Communications Technologies

Revolutionary changes in communications technologies are offering public managers new techniques for obtaining information without surrendering authority. Technologies that have already produced many changes in other realms, ranging from the globalization of businesses to home shopping networks, are now affecting public involvement, too.

The defining characteristic of these technologies is the facilitation of communication. Information can be transmitted more easily, more completely, and more rapidly by means of such telecommunications innovations as computers and modem linkages, which facilitate electronic mail, fax transmissions, and the like. Information that once took hours or days to transport can now be transmitted almost instantaneously. The face-to-face discussions that once required transporting all parties to the same location can now be accomplished by two-way telecommunications technologies.

Interactive television may represent the best example of these new technologies. With interactive television, citizens can observe a public meeting or discussion on their televisions, and then, if they wish, offer personal reactions to that discussion without leaving their living rooms. "Electronic town meetings," as presidential candidate H. Ross Perot advocated, may even offer the promise of creating a "teledemocracy."

Other new technologies include telephone voice-mail systems, electronic computer bulletin boards, and even "multimedia kiosks," which consist of "a personal computer, color screen, laser disk player and other devices enclosed in a cabinet located in a very public place. These systems, connecting to states' or municipalities' central computers, provide integrated access to a range of government information, and some of them allow users to apply for services" (Polilli, 1994, p. 25). Kiosks offer citizens the advantage of obtaining information and access to multiple services at one location. At the same time, the information citizens request through kiosks may be used by government in much the same way as cumulative data on citizen-initiated contacts are used.

The new technologies carry tremendous implications for public involvement. As Barber (1984, p. 274) has speculated in his argument for strengthening American democracy, "The capabilities of the new technology can be used to strengthen civic education, guarantee equal access to information, and tie individuals and institutions into networks that will make real participatory discussion and debate possible across great distances. Thus for the first time we have an opportunity to create artificial town meetings among populations that could not otherwise communicate."

In short, the new technologies could facilitate communication between citizens and government, thereby improving governmental understanding of citizen needs and increasing citizen influence over public programs. At the same time, relevant to the concerns of this chapter, the new technologies could increase the means and ease by which policy makers and public managers can obtain information from the public without necessarily sharing influence. Citizens may be more willing to volunteer information if less effort is required to communicate ideas to government. The artificial town meeting of which Barber wrote, for example, could become a good source of information, without any necessary sharing of authority, as the traditional public meeting could not.

Yet, the prospects for enhanced public involvement through new technologies should not be exaggerated. For one thing, many governments may be unable to afford the substantial new public spending necessary to install these technologies or to adapt them for public involvement. These technologies can be expensive, and many officials may not see the expense as warranted for a public involvement they may still regard as mostly a nuisance.

In addition, these new technologies will bring some of the same problems that plague traditional forms of public involvement. In particular, managers may find that the opinions articulated through new telecommunications technologies are no more representative than traditional citizen-initiated contacts; or, if communication becomes much easier, the opinions communicated by the public may not necessarily reflect much conviction, a complaint often lodged against citizen surveys.

Even with these risks, the new technologies offer considerable promise for the future of public involvement. Public managers should be open to these possibilities, without falling victim to an illusion that new technologies can overcome all of the problems of the old ones.

Comparison

Public managers frequently need information from the public, yet are unwilling to share authority as the price for that information. Either the situation calls for a modified autonomous decision-making approach, in which no authority is shared because public acceptance of the decision is not crucial, or the manager may want information as an initial step in planning decision making on issues for which public acceptance may be sought and authority over the decision eventually shared. The choice of techniques is usually reduced then to those described in this chapter.

To use these techniques to advantage, the public manager must keep in mind the strengths and weaknesses of each. In general, citizen surveys can usually provide the most representative picture of public opinion, but a survey is also a relatively inflexible technique with a limited ability to provide in-depth information. By contrast, consulting with key contacts brings flexibility and the potential for generating in-depth information, but may not accurately represent the opinions of the full public. Citizen-initiated contacts are likely to fall between surveys and key contacts on both dimensions. Too little is yet known about new communication technologies to say how they may fit into this framework.

Choice among these techniques should also be based on an assessment of the situation at hand. Some situations call for more representative information, others for more in-depth insights. In addition, to compensate for the weaknesses of a specific technique, the manager should frequently use more than one technique; or the decision maker may be able to take steps, as Mario Cuomo did in mediating the Forest Hills dispute, to use a technique such as consulting with key contacts in a manner that corrects for its disadvantages.

Only seldom, however, should public involvement be pursued through these techniques alone. The need to obtain more than information from the public usually calls for different or additional techniques, the subject of the next chapter.

Chapter Seven

Involving the Public
to Build Acceptance

More often than not, the impetus for public involvement comes from a need to obtain acceptance as a prerequisite to successful implementation. Fully 85 percent of the cases examined in the reanalysis (see Chapter Three and Appendix A), for example, brought such a need. Successful pursuit of this acceptance requires more extensive public involvement than that described in Chapter Six.

The techniques appropriate in these cases must allow for sharing decision-making authority with the public. This sharing may require difficult personal adjustments by managers and by the public (see Chapter Eight), but only by sharing authority can managers expect to nurture the ownership that underlies acceptance of a decision. The prospect of influence can also help to persuade citizens to give their time to public involvement.

The techniques appropriate for obtaining acceptance also contrast with those discussed in Chapter Six in that they usually bring the public together as a group, rather than drawing information separately from individual citizens. Only by meeting as a group can the public develop a group sense of decision acceptance.

Three principal techniques satisfy these criteria: (1) public meetings, (2) advisory committees, and (3) mediation. Although they are not the only forms of public involvement available for obtaining acceptance, they are the techniques most commonly used toward that end. The remainder of this chapter considers each of these techniques in turn.

Public Meetings

When told to involve the public in making a decision, officials frequently resort to a procedure that was popular long before the contemporary push for increased involvement—the public hearing or public meeting. These meetings probably remain the most common formal procedure for involvement today: "When there is a demand for public involvement in a project or a legislative mandate for such involvement, the knee-jerk reaction is to hold a public hearing" (Heberlein, 1976, p. 199).

The Critique

Even though they are the most popular form of citizen participation, public meetings are also the most maligned form. Critics contend, for one thing, that public meetings do not elicit representative opinions: "The belief that the people involved, as well as the opinions gathered, in public meetings are not representative of the client public or their views has been stated so often that it is now generally accepted" (Gundry and Heberlein, 1984, p. 175).

The problem has several aspects. First, the people who attend public meetings may be atypical of either the general population or any narrower relevant public. Citizen advocates argue that these meetings provide only another forum for established interest groups, "those whose economic stake is large enough to warrant the investment required to make a significant contribution" (Checkoway, 1981, p. 568).

Second, even if attendance at a meeting is representative, the opinions expressed may not be. Of the many people who attend, only a few may be able to speak in the time available, and their opinions may not accurately reflect the feelings of the many. This problem is reflected in the complaint that "public meetings often are too large and unwieldy, thus inhibiting people's ability to express their views and engage in discussion" (The Kettering Foundation, 1991, p. 15).

Third, critics also complain that public meetings seldom permit the public to influence governmental decisions. According to Checkoway (1981, p. 569), "evidence indicates that agency officials may either give cursory consideration to or ignore altogether certain views expressed in hearings." Public meetings may be used only as rituals, providing the appearance but not the reality of public involvement.

The Rebuttal

The criticisms overstate the case against public meetings. Rather than being an intrinsically poor procedure for public involvement, the public meeting may mostly have been poorly managed toward that end. All too often, officials have failed to conceptualize the public meeting as different from the traditional public hearing, the inadequacies of which contributed to the search for new involvement procedures. If carefully planned to overcome these inadequacies, the public meeting can be an excellent means for achieving representative and effective involvement that meets the needs of both the manager and the larger public.

Planning should begin with an assessment of the purpose of the meeting. As Cogan (1992, p. 3) explains, "The purpose of the public meeting may be informational, advisory, decision making, or some combination thereof. The format and structure should be developed only after you have ascertained the reason for the meeting." Answering the questions posed in Chapters Three through Five should clarify that purpose, as well as suggest whether a public meeting is appropriate.

The meeting should also be scheduled at a time and location convenient to interested citizens. It is usually a mistake to schedule a meeting during weekday working hours, because most citizens will have difficulty attending. The meeting should also be well publicized, with special efforts made to get the word to those most likely to be interested. A meeting to discuss limiting the use of road salt in winter months in Madison, Wisconsin, was publicized by announcing the meeting "in local newspapers and on two radio stations. In addition, postcard announcements were sent to aldermen, to people who had appeared at previous meetings on the topic, to neighborhood organizations and environmental groups, and to people who had written letters to newspapers about the program" (Gundry and Heberlein, 1984, p. 177).

When care is given to scheduling and publicity, eventual meeting attendance may prove representative of the relevant publics. In the Wisconsin case, the citizen attendees at the public meeting were very similar to the general public. As Gundry and Heberlein (1984, p. 181) concluded, "Although meeting participants may differ on some demographic characteristics, their opinions do not seriously mislead the planner who is attempting to ascertain the prevailing opinion among the general public."

To further enhance representative attendance, planners might use "citizen panels," a recent innovation on public meetings (see Crosby, Kelly, and Schaefer, 1986). In this approach, citizens are randomly selected, and then paid a modest stipend to participate in deliberating an issue. Random selection, especially when stratified to ensure representation of relevant publics, increases the likelihood of representative attendance. Better representation comes at some cost, however, since stipends may be in the range of $100 per person per day.

Running the Meeting

Attracting representative attendance is only half the battle. Care must also be given to running the meeting in order to achieve the often competing goals of representative articulation of opinions and effective closure on the issue (that is, either a decision or a sense of the public's preferences).

Various techniques are available to enhance the voicing of opinions at public meetings. In one popular approach, attendees are divided into smaller "focus groups," each of which discusses the issue and then reports back to the meeting as a whole. This methodology is often used in conjunction with public meetings to facilitate defining opinions for each of the small groups.

This approach, also sometimes called the "workshop technique," is useful for maximizing the sense citizens have of participating in the public meeting. "Workshops usually interest participants because they can do something other than sit and listen. . . . This technique provides an excellent opportunity for those with opposing viewpoints to establish a dialogue, whether or not they reach agreement" (Hendee and others, 1976, p. 131). The procedure can be "costly and time-consuming for the agency," however. Obtaining trained focus group leaders can itself be expensive. In addition, if continued too long, the workshop approach "may tend to weed out participation by all but the most avid individuals and interest groups" (Hendee and others, 1976, p. 131). As with other involvement techniques, the manager should endeavor not to ask more of citizens than they are able to give.

This approach has been used with success in recent years by a number of school systems, including the Savannah-Chatham County Schools in Georgia (Donald, 1994). The school system annually holds a Community Priorities Workshop, a one-day session in which more than one hundred community residents are asked to discuss their feelings about the area's schools. Those invited include teachers, students, and parents, along with business, government, and other community leaders. The first half of the day is devoted to attendees meeting in small focus groups to define their concerns. All attendees then meet as one group in the afternoon to define five or six major goals for the schools in the upcoming year.

When participants at a public meeting meet as a single large group, the manager may want to place responsibility for running the meeting in the hands of a trained facilitator. A facilitator is someone trained in group process skills who works with a group to "increase its effectiveness by improving its process" and "to solve problems and make decisions" (Schwarz, 1994, pp. 5–6).

The facilitator is a neutral outsider who brings no preconceptions to the issues. As such, the facilitator should not be a member of the group—neither agency staff nor a representative of the public—and should not take sides on the issue. Rather, "the role of the facilitator is to stimulate, organize, and synthesize the thinking of the group so that it can reach consensus. Sometimes an agreement to disagree may be the best that can be attained, but the facilitator helps the group go as far as it can, without ridiculing, or ignoring anyone's point of view" (Cogan, 1992, p. 13). These are tasks that the manager, by virtue of having a stake in the issue, cannot perform effectively. Indeed, the manager who attempts to serve as facilitator invites unwanted and unnecessary problems. (For more on the role of facilitators, see Schwarz, 1994; on facilitators in public meetings in particular, see Cogan, 1992, pp. 13–17.) Conversely, the process may work more smoothly if the manager understands how facilitation and negotiation work (see Chapter Eight; also Fisher and Ury, 1983).

The manager (or facilitator) might consider other techniques to avoid domination of a meeting by a few vocal citizens. As one possibility, after open discussion, ballots or questionnaires might be used to ensure that everyone has an opportunity to register opinions.

Achieving representative participation at public meetings will go a long way toward increasing citizen influence. That influence ultimately depends on public officials deciding to heed the opinions citizens express, and those officials are more likely to heed opinions that appear to represent the true public sentiments. A case in point is when the public participated in a representative manner in thirty public hearings on proposed highway improvements in four states. "Highway department representatives in all four states indicated that 90 percent of the proposed highway projects had been changed as a result of citizen involvement in the hearing process. The magnitude of such changes varied, but vocal citizen opposition to one project in Nebraska actually halted the project" (Kihl, 1985, p. 198).

When to Use This Technique

Under the right circumstances, "public hearings are simple to run, can be implemented quickly, and provide results" (Gundry and Heberlein, 1984, p. 181). The key is knowing what those circumstances are.

To begin with, public meetings should be used principally when managers wish to exchange information with citizens. "Exchange" implies two-way communication, by which citizens and managers inform each other, rather than one-way communication, by which managers inform citizens but are deaf to citizen reactions. In short, public meetings ordinarily should not be used unless citizen information is likely to affect a decision. Such sharing of decision-making authority is the necessary price for what the manager asks the public to give to the meeting.

Using public meetings for more extensive purposes is difficult, but not impossible. Public meetings can sometimes be used in actual decision making, especially when there is a "yes-no" question (for example, should we undertake this program or not?). More elaborate decision making with public meetings is also possible, but it demands a structured series of meetings, and multiple meetings can bring a fall-off in attendance, threatening representativeness. The public meeting is too unwieldy a mechanism to use for decision making that must be elaborate, representative, and expeditious.

Public meetings work best, too, when the relevant public is at least partially unorganized. Organized groups can see an implied challenge to their legitimacy in the holding of an "open" public meeting. The manager who sees a need to hold a meeting anyway may want to avoid that implied insult. Municipal officials have often solved this problem with neighborhood organizations by expanding the regular meetings of those organizations into broader public meetings.

Managers need not rule out occasional use of public meetings for informational purposes only. Many citizen advocates (for example, Checkoway, 1981, p. 571) frown on this possibility, but it is sometimes warranted. Consider, in particular, a situation in which the manager sees a decision as largely dictated by technical and professional criteria, with public acceptance not needed for implementation, but public involvement is required by law. A public meeting may then be the best means to meet the legal requirement for involvement without inviting the extensive participation that could build an expectation of substantial citizen influence. If this approach is taken, however, the manager should be candid in explaining, to the extent legally permitted, that the hearing is being held only to inform, not to solicit opinions that might influence a decision. In addition, use of public meetings for this nominal citizen participation should be the exception, because frequent use of public meetings in this manner in the past has helped to discredit the technique.

It is unfortunate that public meetings have been discredited. As this discussion has indicated, public meetings continue to hold value as a means for engaging public involvement. That promise can be realized, however, only if managers recognize when and how to use these meetings for both public involvement and public influence.

Advisory Committees

Public involvement can also be pursued through advisory committees composed of representatives from interested groups, including businesses, labor unions, and agency staff, as well as citizens groups. This is, in effect, a "republican" form of involvement in that participation, rather than being open to all comers, is restricted to a small number of individuals who are expected to represent the interests of larger publics.

Using advisory committees as a form of public involvement, though hardly a new idea, has grown in popularity in recent times. The principal impetus for the growth came from the many federal initiatives of the late 1960s and 1970s—the poverty programs, in particular—that required that committees representing affected interests be appointed to advise on program operation. In addition, public officials have sometimes formed these committees on their own in the hope of gaining a better understanding of public sentiments.

Advantages and Disadvantages

The advisory committee has several advantages. First, when multiple groups have stakes in an issue, decisions may be more easily reached through an advisory committee than through any alternative approach, such as public meetings or separate negotiations with each of the interested groups. Finding a solution acceptable to all may be difficult and time consuming whatever approach is used, but less so with an advisory committee, assuming its membership can be kept manageable. The optimal size may be no more than fifteen members—large enough to represent a variety of interests, small enough for everyone to be involved without decision making dragging on interminably.

A second advantage is that the honor of advisory committee membership encourages thinking on behalf of the larger community, rather than only as a representative of a particular interest. This can facilitate the shaping of a decision supportive of the public interest.

Finally, as the first two advantages imply, an advisory committee can also serve as an excellent vehicle for building public acceptance of a decision.

Conversely, there are risks to this approach. For one, committee members could unite in opposition to agency goals or quality requirements, producing a recommendation at odds with what the manager believes. The manager should be able to minimize this risk, however, by following the guidelines described in Chapter Five (for example, do not use an advisory committee if you *expect* the public to be united in opposition to agency goals).

The greater risks have to do with how well committee members represent the public. The membership itself might be viewed by particular groups as not representing their interests; or, since committee work can demand substantial time, some committee members may not participate fully, perhaps leaving important groups unrepresented in deliberations. If for either reason the committee is viewed as unrepresentative, one or more constituent groups may reject any eventual committee decision. The committee's recommendation will then have failed to gain the acceptance that was a principal purpose in creating the committee.

These risks can be minimized if care is taken in appointing committee members. Some managers may be tempted to appoint "average citizens," hoping that their lack of an organized group affiliation will promote a disinterested, unbiased outlook. The evidence suggests, however, that the better committee members come from among the leaders of those organizations. These leaders are more likely to be accepted as legitimate representatives of the relevant publics, and their experience in positions of community responsibility makes them "most likely to display the type of broad orientation conducive to effective decision making" and less likely to fall into a narrow pursuit of self-interest (Cole, 1981, p. 59). With their stronger sense of civic responsibility, these leaders are likely to participate actively in the committee's work, whereas the average citizen could prove more uninterested than disinterested. The endorsement of these leaders also enhances the likelihood of the committee's recommendation proving acceptable to constituent groups.

This strategy is more difficult to follow when the manager wants to represent an unorganized public. The manager might then try to choose individuals who have demonstrated a continuing interest in the issue, such as by attending previous public meetings. Elections offer another means for selecting these representatives, although the historically low turnout rates for advisory committee elections implies that they can be more democratic in appearance than in reality.

Pressures to represent a broad range of interests will sometimes force officials to appoint a committee too large for easy decision making. A committee numbering more than fifteen members can lend itself to lengthy and unproductive discussions. If a large membership cannot be avoided, the manager might divide the group into subcommittees, each charged with deliberating a specific issue before reporting back to the full committee.

No selection procedure assures that members will adapt readily to the advisory committee task. That being the case, managers should provide training to aid in this adaptation. Training sessions can help, as Cole (1981, p. 58) has noted, by providing citizen representatives "with opportunities to become familiar with the terminology and jargon used by professionals." Viewed from the manager's perspective, training can also educate committee members on important quality requirements, thereby helping to protect necessary managerial prerogatives. Training should not be viewed as a one-way process, however. Managers and agency staff must expect—and plan—to use the process to learn about the concerns of committee members, too.

As with public meetings, managers should also consider using trained facilitators with advisory committees when the committee as a whole must debate and resolve an issue. The manager who has a stake in the issue, especially a controversial issue, may have difficulty moving the committee to resolution.

When to Use This Technique

Advisory committees work best under these circumstances: First, the relevant public should include, at a minimum, two or more organized groups, including citizens groups and other interested groups, as well as perhaps an unorganized public. The advisory committee then offers a means to represent each of the groups in a manner still amenable to decision making, as illustrated in Case 7.1 (adapted from Friedman, 1978). By contrast, an advisory committee is usually a poor idea when the relevant public is either entirely unorganized (the selection of "representative" members is too difficult) or limited to one organized group (the group itself can advise).

Case 7.1

Advisory Committees in Regulatory Decision Making

The federal Food and Drug Administration (FDA) has the responsibility for evaluating new drugs prior to their introduction on the market. It can be a difficult responsibility, because the FDA's in-house staff is too limited to provide the scientific expertise necessary to evaluate the many new drugs proposed each year. Nor can that staff by itself compensate for "the absence of formal inputs from industry and consumer interests" (Friedman, 1978, p. 206).

This is a situation that calls for significant public involvement. Such involvement can compensate for inadequate information by generating both scientific information on how the quality requirements apply to particular drugs and information on industry and consumer preferences. Involvement is also needed to gain the acceptance of interested groups—industry and consumer groups as well as scientists—which is a prerequisite to successful implementation of FDA decisions. That acceptance could not be assumed if those groups were excluded from decision making. At the same time, public involvement must be limited to ensure that the FDA's decisions respect the essential quality requirements (drug safety and effectiveness) and problem structure (the FDA ordinarily has no option to redesign drugs).

Since the relevant public consists of multiple organized groups and unorganized consumers, the need for public involvement may best be satisfied by the use of advisory committees. Bringing representatives of the various groups together in a committee should not threaten the necessary quality requirements, because all groups are likely to support the FDA goals of drug safety and effectiveness.

Moreover, the task has enough intrinsic significance to entice members to participate.

Appraising the situation accurately, the FDA during the 1960s and early 1970s formed a variety of advisory committees "to provide an opportunity to all interested parties to make inputs to the decision making process." By 1974, sixty-six such committees were active. "Structurally, most of the committees consist of nine members, seven of whom are professionals in the field of the committee's subject matter; one member represents industry and one represents consumers. Only the seven scientific members have voting privileges. Scientific members are selected by the FDA commissioner on the basis of nominations submitted by interested professional groups and individuals. Industry and consumer representatives are appointed by the commissioner on the basis of nominations from industry and consumer organizations" (p. 208).

By most accounts, the committees have worked well. In the judgment of FDA staff members, the "committees provided a source of knowledge not otherwise available," meeting the FDA's need for more information. Moreover, the committees also "provide a cloak of legitimacy through their expert knowledge," and "provide credibility for the FDA in the medical field," thereby enhancing the likelihood of successful implementation of committee decisions (p. 211).

The committees also appear to have increased public influence over agency decisions. When asked, approximately three-fourths of the committee members reported that their opinions had significantly influenced agency decisions. Among consumer representatives alone, "two-thirds of the respondents thought that consumer interests were listened to by their panels a great deal" (p. 209). The relatively small, nine-member committee size probably helped by limiting the number of participants in each committee's deliberations.

The FDA has not been able to avoid all of the pitfalls of the advisory committee approach. As might be expected, outside groups have questioned the quality of representation provided by the committees. Consumer groups have been the most vocal, often contending that the FDA has selected consumer representatives who "were not tough minded individuals who could ask penetrating questions." These groups have also sometimes characterized the entire committee structure as inherently biased because "consumer organizations have neither manpower nor resources to support their representatives and provide them with the knowledge base available to industry" (p. 212).

***

Second, an advisory committee is also a poor idea if the manager believes that committee members agree among themselves on goals, but disagree with agency goals. An advisory committee in this situation could increase opposition to agency goals. The committee approach should be reserved for situations in which different segments of the public either agree with the agency's goals or disagree among themselves.

Third, advisory committees should be used only on important issues in which the manager is willing to share substantial decision-making power. Creating an advisory committee implies that the task will be significant. If the issue is seen as unimportant or the committee's authority as too circumscribed, committee members could turn against the agency or the program, either opposing the manager or abandoning the process.

Mediation

An increasing number of issues that call for public involvement have proved so intractable that they cannot be resolved by any of the conventional public involvement techniques. The goal disagreements between the interested parties are too great, the distrust between those parties too strong, or the number of interested parties too many. For one or more of those reasons, it becomes fruitless to seek an acceptable decision using key contacts, public hearings, advisory committees, or almost any other procedure. Reaching a decision may then require mediation, in which a third party, usually a professional mediator who has no allegiance to any of the parties with a stake in the issue, intercedes to seek a resolution.

Mediation is often confused with facilitation, and in fact the two techniques have many similarities. To begin with, "both involve intervention by a neutral third party who is acceptable to the clients and who has no decision-making authority" (Schwarz, 1994, p. 12). Both also require group process skills.

Mediation differs from facilitation in important ways, however. The crucial difference is that mediation usually occurs after a conflict has reached an impasse, while facilitation often begins earlier. In addition, the two techniques usually have different objectives. Where the goal of mediation is to resolve a particular conflict, facilitation is more often designed to improve the process of decision making. Finally, because mediation begins at the point of impasse, "mediators exert greater control over the process than facilitators do. The mediator controls the process by determining who should talk when and by having the disputants follow certain ground rules and a set procedure and discuss the conflict in a specific order" (Schwarz, 1994, p. 13).

Mediation's Growing Popularity

Although mediation has a long history as a technique for resolving labor-management disputes, its use for public involvement is relatively new, spanning less than two decades. In that time, usage has increased rapidly, especially with environmental issues. According to one study (Bingham, 1985, p. 3), as late as the end of 1977 only nine environmental disputes in the United States had been mediated, but "another 9 were mediated in 1978, and 18 more were mediated in 1979. By mid 1984, mediators had been involved in over 160 disputes." By the early 1980s, the use of mediation had spread to other issues, including economic development and inter-governmental relations (see Sullivan, 1984; Carlson, 1983).

All of these issues share two characteristics. First, all of them have featured conflict between two or more nongovernmental groups. Mediations often find government as a third-party observer or additional interest in conflicts that involve primarily these non-governmental groups. Second, the competing groups have usually included at least one of the new breed of citizen groups, such as an environmental or neighborhood organization, which have prolif-erated since the 1960s.

This latter trait is crucial for explaining the growing popularity of mediation for public involvement. The new role of citizen groups in American public life has promoted mediation first by cre-ating the "relative power between the parties" necessary for medi-ation to be an attractive option (Cormick and Patten, 1977, p. 4). Submitting a dispute to a third party makes little sense if one of the first two parties has power sufficient to dictate the decision. Medi-ation becomes attractive only when neither side can overpower the other.

The rise of citizen groups has also frequently led to "an impasse between the parties," a second condition conducive to the use of mediation (Cormick and Patten, 1977, p. 4). Across a variety of policy areas, long-dominant established interests have failed to rec-ognize the need to share power with emerging citizen groups, often attempting instead to ignore citizen input, a tactic that also increases the likelihood of impasse.

For mediation to be desirable, however, the opposing sides must move a step beyond impasse, reaching the point of being "prepared to compromise" (Cormick and Patten, 1977, p. 4). This third con-dition takes time to develop, which helps to explain why media-tion did not become a popular option in the early years of the new public involvement. Mediation emerged as an attractive option only in the late 1970s, once established interests had accepted the new power of citizen groups and once citizen groups had become more willing to compromise; it has been used increasingly ever since.

Where these conditions hold, it often falls to government to consider mediation. The public manager or other official must then consider both whether the competing parties are prepared for mediation and whether government, if it also has preferences on the issue, satisfies the prerequisites for mediation as well.

Mediation with the Public

Under the appropriate conditions, mediation can be an effective option for public involvement in dispute resolution. For one thing, mediation can enhance the likelihood of agreement. Bingham (1985, p. 7) found that "agreements were reached in 78 percent" of the environmental disputes in which mediation was used, a rate probably much higher than what could have been anticipated from the traditional alternative of letting a court decide.

Second, resolutions reached through mediation may be qualitatively superior to what would be possible through any other procedure. Most notably, litigated settlements are notorious for leaving both sides unhappy. Mediated settlements are more likely to satisfy both sides because, as is seldom true with a court decision, both sides must accept the outcome before it constitutes a settlement.

Government officials may like mediation because necessary quality requirements and problem structure can be protected. Mediators encourage participants to take care in identifying their interests, such as quality requirements, to assure that those interests will be recognized in any solution.

Third, mediation also enhances the chance that an eventual agreement will be implemented, rather than stall along the way. Where mediation has been used in site-specific environmental disputes—disputes focusing on a particular project or plan—80 percent of the agreements were fully implemented and 13 percent were at least partially implemented. Agreements on policy-level disputes, which involve questions of state or national environmental policy, proved more difficult, with only 41 percent fully implemented and 18 percent partially implemented. Even those rates are impressive, however, given that policy-level agreements usually must be ratified by legislatures and/or executives, seldom an easy process (Bingham, 1985).

Mediation has its costs. Mediators themselves can be expensive, a fact too often overlooked in the early years of experimentation. "During the first decade in which mediators have helped parties to environmental disputes resolve issues directly with one another, the mediators' services have been paid for principally by foundation grants. Corporate donations, government contracts, in-kind support from citizens groups and public interest organizations, and fees have made up the rest. For the most part, however, the mediators' services have been free of charge to the parties. The question of how these services will continue to be paid is pressing" (Bingham, 1985, p. 7). A partial answer to the question could be found in special funds that have been created to support the citizens' share. The governmental share of the cost, however, must usually come from public coffers, which may already be overcommitted.

When to Use This Technique

Mediation is limited by being an option in only a narrow range of circumstances. As already explained, the opposing parties to a dispute must have comparable power, their dispute must have reached impasse, and they must be prepared to compromise. From the manager's perspective, acceptance of a decision should be essential to successful implementation. As well, the representatives who will speak for the opposing sides in the mediation must have the authority to make a decision that can resolve the conflict (Cormick and Patten, 1977). When these conditions are met, mediation can be an effective technique for dispute resolution with public involvement, as illustrated by the Port Townsend siting dispute introduced in Chapter Four, continued here in Case 7.2 (adapted from Talbot, 1983).

———•———

Case 7.2

Siting the Port Townsend Terminal, Part II

Mediation succeeded where other approaches had failed to resolve the Port Townsend dispute. To recap, the marine division of the state of Washington's department of transportation wanted to develop a new ferry landing and terminal in the Olympic Peninsula community. An initial plan had to be abandoned when a large, previously unorganized segment of the community mobilized in opposition.

As the impasse over where to put the terminal dragged into a third year, "pressures to resolve the dispute grew" as the "delays and traffic snarls caused by the old landing were getting worse" (Talbot, 1983, p. 84). Finally, in March 1979 a state senator asked the Institute for Environmental Mediation for assistance. The institute asked George Yount, an intern on its staff, to examine the possibility of mediation.

When Yount began interviewing Port Townsend residents in April of that year, he found a situation seemingly well suited to mediation. The dispute was at an impasse, and the continuing stalemate implied a relative balance of power between the opposing sides, thereby satisfying the first two conditions for mediation. Perhaps most important, the principals in the dispute were "sufficiently tired of fighting to be prepared to get on with building a ferry landing somewhere" (p. 85), thus satisfying the third condition. Finally, the parties able to make the decision—the newcomers to the community, the traditional residents, and the state—could all be involved in the mediation, satisfying the fourth necessary condition.

Having determined that mediation might work, Yount began to assemble the small group of residents who would be involved.

"These were the townfolk who did not fall into simple categories of established or new residents. In many cases, they were people who had not taken a position on the ferry, but who nonetheless had opinions. . . . Interviews narrowed the list of town leaders to nine people who said they would participate in mediation and who . . . would have their agreement on a ferry site accepted by just about everyone else in town" (p. 85).

Yount began the mediation sessions in late 1979 by seeking agreement on ground rules, including a rule that the committee's ultimate site recommendation would be unanimous. The next few sessions focused on setting the criteria by which possible sites would be evaluated. Consistent with the principles of negotiation, Yount was asking the opposing sides to define their "interests" rather than "positions": "There were the state's needs for quick traffic movement, sufficient parking, and size. A total of about two acres was needed. It was also necessary to pick a proposal that could be realized with the available funds, about $3 million. Most of the panel preferred the landing to be kept in or close to downtown so that passengers would continue to use downtown shops. On the other hand, some on the panel were concerned about pollution and the effects of traffic vibration on the older buildings" (pp. 86–87). Only after setting those criteria did the committee begin to evaluate particular sites. The process then bogged down, with one participant complaining: "By the fifth meeting . . . it was nothing but arguments and opinions, and we weren't getting anywhere" (p. 87).

To many of the participants, Yount appeared at this stage to be doing little "aside from opening and closing the meetings, raising questions, and calling occasional coffee breaks." In reality, he was following the principle, as he explained later, that, "part of mediation means letting people express their anger and frustration," especially early in the process. At the same time, he was looking "continually for areas where they can agree. That begins with setting dates or times for the meetings, and then moves on to listening to what they say, pointing out where they concur, and getting them accustomed to agreeing on things" (pp. 87–88).

That approach led eventually to a solution on which everyone could agree. One of the committee members proposed an entirely new approach involving the creation of "a two-acre landing over the water, rather than using existing shoreline." The proposal "had a potential for future expansion and required no acquisition or demolition" (p. 88). After extensive discussion and some modification, the committee unanimously endorsed the proposal in March 1980.

The results were not an unqualified success. Conflict over the site ended as all sides accepted the decision, but budget limitations prevented the state from beginning construction until June 1982, and then at a projected cost of $6 million, twice the original estimate. In addition, "suspicions and occasional bad feelings still marked the relationship between some new and old residents" (p. 89).

Use of mediation as a public involvement procedure also requires that a "public decision" approach be appropriate. Only with that approach does the manager surrender significant decision-making authority to other actors (relevant citizen groups, industry groups, other concerned parties, and the mediator) as mediation demands. Any approach implying less sharing of authority, such as consultation with the public, gives too little power to the mediation. The manager still retains some authority by being able to stipulate quality requirements as part of agency interests. In the Port Townsend case, for example, the state asserted its "needs for quick traffic movement, sufficient parking," and a two-acre size (Talbot, 1983, pp. 86–87).

Mediation is not limited to any particular type of public. It may be easiest to implement where the relevant public is comprised of only a small number of organized groups, since participants might then be selected from the groups' leaders. Selection of representatives becomes more difficult if there is a relevant unorganized public, but a mediator can utilize techniques such as the interview process George Yount used to select committee members for the Port Townsend mediation.

Mediation can also become more difficult when there are many organized groups or interests, but the sheer number of groups need not prevent success if all parties have incentives to reach agreement. A mediation of development questions related to the Appalachian Trail corridor in Vermont, for example, involved twenty-five interest groups and two ski development corporations (Lobel, 1992). Yet, because every party had an incentive, the mediation succeeded after only six months of negotiation.

Conclusion

The discussions in this and the previous chapter can be summarized in the form of recommendations about which form of public involvement may be most appropriate in any given situation. The matrix in Table 7.1 shows the form of public involvement most appropriate for particular publics and decision-making approaches.

In practice, public managers should seldom restrict themselves to one technique of public involvement in resolving an issue. Public managers must consider the requirements of the specific issue, as well as keeping an eye on how those requirements change as the issue develops, in order to involve the public in a manner most likely to improve the effectiveness of public management.

Table 7.1   A Matrix Guide to Forms of Public Involvement.

Style of Decision Making	The Nature of the Public			
	One Organized Group	Multiple Organized Groups	Unorganized Public	Complex Public*
Modified Autonomous Managerial	Key contacts	Key contacts	Citizen survey/ citizen contacts	Key contacts/ survey/ citizen contacts
Segmented Public Consultation	Key contacts	Contacts/ series of meetings	Citizen survey	Citizen survey/ meetings
Unitary Public Consultation	Meeting(s) with group	Advisory committee/ series of meetings	Series of public meetings	Advisory committee and/or meetings
Public Decision	Negotiate with group	Negotiate with advisory committee	Series of public meetings	Advisory committee/ public meetings

*Complex public=some combination of organized and unorganized groups

Chapter Eight

Building Strong Relationships with Citizens

No phase of public involvement may pose more difficulties for public managers than simply getting started. Managers and publics often enter this involvement as virtual strangers who must learn quickly how to work with each other. Recognizing how much authority should be shared with the public and in what format greatly enhances the chances of success, but the manager and the public must also work within that framework to build what Fisher and Brown (1988, p. xiii) term "a good 'working' relationship—one that is able to deal well with differences."

The purpose of this chapter is to explore how to build this good working relationship. The chapter first examines how Fisher and Brown's advice on "building a relationship that gets to yes" can help managers in building a relationship with the public. The second part of the chapter explains the special importance to this relationship of creating an informed public. A final section considers the potential value of providing assistance to citizen groups.

Guidelines for Building Good Relationships

Before initiating a relationship with any public, the manager should be sure that the effort is warranted. That requires a determination, based on criteria explained in earlier chapters, that there is a significant role for the public to play. It also requires assurance that the necessary governmental leaders are committed to that role.

The Prerequisite: Leadership Commitment

As a general rule, public involvement should not be invited without first obtaining the commitment of the governmental leaders who must approve of the results of that involvement. These leaders may be either the top managers in the agency or elected officials to whom those managers report. In either case, these leaders must be committed to both the process and the outcomes of public involvement, understanding in advance how the agency's authority is to be shared with the public.

This conclusion emerges clearly from research on all manner of organizational change as well as from research on public involvement in particular. For example, a recent assessment of a variety of Management by Objectives (MBO) efforts concluded: "The MBO process spreads from the top down. If top management does not personally participate in the process, then the system is half-hearted and ultimately should not succeed" (Rodgers and Hunter, 1992, pp. 36–37). Analysts of public involvement also have concluded that public involvement initiatives seldom work without "the commitment of individual administrators to make them work" (Berry, Portney, and Thomson, 1993, pp. 43–44); or, as Cogan (1992, p. 7) said of public meetings, "citizens endure all manner of inconvenience and forgive those inevitable glitches if they believe in their leaders. Conversely, the most ideal setting and circumstances cannot make up for inadequate leadership."

Often, only the manager's commitment is necessary. In policy implementation, managers commonly hold ultimate authority, if such authority is specified within the constraints of the source legislation. Managers must then be sure only of their own commitment to public involvement and to any sharing of authority.

In some cases, that authority is shared with other public officials, including the manager's elected superiors, other managers in the same agency, or managers of other agencies with overlapping programs. The manager must then be sure that these other officials buy into the involvement before it begins. Optimally, these officials should also participate in the involvement process, both to ensure that their ideas are heard and to cement their commitment to the process.

A public manager may on rare occasions initiate public involvement without first obtaining leadership commitment. Events could unfold so rapidly that a manager senses an urgency to working with the public that does not allow for obtaining advance commitment; or, operating as a "guerrilla in the bureaucracy" (Needleman and Needleman, 1974), the manager may feel impelled to mobilize the public in order to get a message to governmental leaders.

This is a risky choice. The manager's own commitment may lend the necessary influence to the involvement process, perhaps eventually winning over other leaders, but the manager also risks alienating those leaders, as well as the public, should those leaders balk at recommendations that come from the public's involvement.

The Goal and Basic Strategy

Once leadership commitment is obtained, the manager can turn to building a working relationship with the public. Given the likelihood of differences of opinion in any relationship—and certainly in a relationship between the public and a public agency—the relationship can be said to work only to the extent that the parties are able to deal well with their differences. Consistent with Fisher and Brown (1988, p. 3), success here is defined as including both outcomes that serve the interests of all parties in the relationship and good feelings about how those outcomes were achieved.

According to Fisher and Brown (1988, p. 16), to reach that goal the parties must first "disentangle relationship issues from substantive issues," separating process issues—how disagreements are handled—from outcome issues—what agreements are reached. This principle is crucial to public involvement, in which process issues can be the core issues.

Second, the parties should be "unconditionally constructive" (Fisher and Brown, 1988, p. 24); that is, any party wanting to build a working relationship should be constructive toward that end independent of what other parties do. The behavior of other parties should not be ignored, nor should personal interests be sacrificed; to the contrary, this is a "risk averse" strategy, by which each party does "only those things that are good both for the relationship and . . . for us" (Fisher and Brown, 1988, pp. 37–38).

Elements of a Good Working Relationship

Within this general strategy, there are a number of principles that should also be observed. First, the parties need to balance emotion with reason, giving a role to both (Fisher and Brown, 1988, p. 43). Managers working with the public may err on the side of reason by attempting to suppress the voicing of emotions. The better strategy is to ensure that emotions are expressed, without allowing them to become the sole focus of the relationship.

A second principle is to understand how the other side perceives issues. As Fisher and Brown (1988, pp. 65–66) have noted, "The problem itself may exist only because of a misunderstanding," which "creates a problem in our heads that is not there in reality." Closely related to understanding is communication, a third principle. Two of the ways communication can fail are familiar to students of public involvement:

1. *"We assume there is no need to talk."* Public managers have too often assumed no need to talk, erroneously concluding that the public would acquiesce to decisions made by managers.

2. *"We communicate in one direction: we 'tell' people."* Too often, public managers have invited public involvement only to "tell" the public what government will do, permitting no communication from the public. Unfortunately, "not much

'public hearing' goes on at the typical public hearing" (Kemmis, 1990, as cited in Stivers, 1994).

Achieving effective communication in public involvement requires that managers be good listeners, that is, facilitators who help others to communicate their ideas (see Stivers, 1994).

A fourth key to building this relationship is reliability, being "wholly trustworthy" but "not wholly trusting" (Fisher and Brown, 1988, pp. 107–110). Given how often citizen groups have perceived governmental agencies as unreliable, public managers must work all the harder to be trustworthy when working with the public. Behavior should be predictable, not erratic; communication should be careful, not careless; and promises should not be lightly made.

A fifth principle is that efforts toward resolving conflict should emphasize "persuasion, not coercion" (Fisher and Brown, 1988, p. 132). Seldom can citizens be coerced, but they may be persuaded.

Acceptance is the final key. As Fisher and Brown (1988, p. 153) have explained, "if I do want a working relationship with you, I will have to accept you as someone with whom to work." Acceptance does not require agreement with the other side's views, but those views must be respected and the other side treated as an equal. Citizen groups must be accepted as legitimate participants in decision making.

The Need for an Informed Public

"The foundation of any program to prevent and resolve public controversy must be an informed public" (Connor, 1988, p. 250). Yet, representatives of the public may come to an involvement process with relatively little information on the issues to be discussed. They may need background education before they can participate intelligently.

The need to educate the public has often been overlooked. Barber (1984, p. 154) complained about many governmental efforts to involve the public in decision making: "They overwhelm people with the least tractable problems of mass society . . . and then carp at their uncertainty or indecisiveness or the simple-mindedness with which they muddle through to a decision. But what general would shove rifles into the hands of civilians, hurry them off to battle, and then call them cowards when they are overrun by the enemy?"

Approaches to Educating the Public

To achieve this need, managers must consider early in any public involvement whether education may be needed. Education ordinarily works best when closely linked to a process in which the public will have influence, such as when agency officials or other experts make presentations at the beginning of a meeting in which public advice will be sought on what action to take on an issue. In Rock Hill, South Carolina, for example, consultants were hired to make "expert presentations on historic preservation, urban development, public art, theater design, greenways (open space) development, and landscape design" to groups of citizens who were advising on a citywide strategic plan (Wheeland, 1993, p. 68).

The vehicles for educating publics can be as diverse as the manager's imagination. Newspapers can be encouraged to assist by publishing special "think" pieces or by carrying short questionnaires for readers to complete and return. Radio and television can be encouraged to devote public affairs programming to the issue. Any of these techniques can both educate the public and increase interest in the issue.

Education has sometimes been pursued through processes that are not tied directly to decision making. In Connecticut, several municipalities created "study circles" to discuss general questions of citizen involvement in municipal affairs. Each circle consisted of a mix of municipal officials, civic leaders, and other citizens, numbering no more than twenty in all. Rather than debating a pressing issue, members discussed general questions about citizenship, including "the ideal meaning of citizenship" and "the quality of citizenship in America," before planning a citizenship program for the community. These experiments appear to have increased public interest and involvement (Sembor, 1992).

When public involvement becomes ongoing, some mechanisms for educating the public can be institutionalized. Many municipalities either send monthly newsletters to residents or provide funds for neighborhood groups to prepare and mail their own newsletters. The city of St. Paul has an "early notification system" that stipulates what neighborhoods need to be told about municipal deliberations and when they must be told (Berry, Portney, Thomson, 1993, pp. 60–61).

Whatever mechanisms are used, managers must ensure that education does not degenerate into government telling citizens what should be done. One way to avoid that pitfall is by keeping in mind that any education should be reciprocal. For public involvement to be effective, public managers must learn from the public. Managers' learning may not come easily, however, since it usually occurs only through unstructured, on-the-job training, involving repeated trial and error.

The Learning Process

When first working with each other, public managers and citizens should, in fact, recognize the need for a gradual learning process on both sides. Although formal educational mechanisms are useful, the informal processes may prove at least as important, as Case 8.1 (adapted from Thomas, 1986) illustrates.

Case 8.1

The Long Learning Process in Cincinnati

The increasing involvement of community councils with municipal government in Cincinnati in the 1970s and 1980s added at least four new elements to municipal decision making. For the city to continue to run effectively, its administrators had to learn to work with these elements in making decisions.

The most obvious change was a substantial increase in the number of decision makers and agendas. As one city official said, "There are many more agendas on the table that you have to deal with" (Thomas, 1986, p. 98). The second element was that it was often unclear which of the would-be participants and agendas warranted more or less attention. Managers were uncertain about who, if anyone, particular self-proclaimed community "representatives" actually represented. The third element was in the agendas, which differed from traditional agendas in that many communities now wanted a role in municipal decision making because they disagreed with earlier decisions. Finally, having sometimes been ignored or manipulated by the city, many communities brought distrust to the table, creating the potential for difficult deliberations.

Judging from their comments, Cincinnati's administrators underwent an extended, unstructured learning process that eventually enabled most of them to cope effectively with these new elements. They learned, for one thing, to listen more. One administrator said with a smile that he had learned to have ears bigger than his mouth in order to understand community priorities. To enhance this listening, many administrators reported regular departmental efforts to stay in touch with the community councils.

As they listened, these administrators learned how to determine who particular groups and leaders actually represented. Those determinations often required a kind of triangulation utilizing such techniques as requesting membership lists, observing attendance at meetings of particular groups, holding public meetings open to all comers, and the like (see Chapter Four).

Administrators also had to learn to be patient in the face of initial hostility. Working and sharing authority with a particular community usually reduced distrust over time, with the community becoming more cooperative. As a health department official said of progress made with once-militant low-income communities, "They come in less with the intent to just beat you up" (p. 99).

Conversely, a lack of patience with that hostility can exacerbate problems. It may be more than coincidence that the Cincinnati administrator who complained most loudly about difficulties with community involvement was the same man who said of facility siting questions: "If a community group starts giving you too much difficulty . . . we can just say, 'We'll go some place else'" (p. 99).

Finally, many administrators had to learn how to bargain and build consensus. One administrator, a recent arrival from a less neighborhood-oriented city, described Cincinnati as having a different brand of politics, in that "you have to build a consensus, have to build a constituency for any decision" (p. 99). Building consensus becomes possible only if the administrator is willing to bend and make trade-offs.

Bargaining does not come easily to those administrators who, believing in the sanctity of the politics-administration dichotomy, believe that they know best what is good for the community. Such a belief was implicit in a department head's complaint that the community councils "can stop through the political process actions which we might feel are actually in their own best interest" (p. 99). In this case, what looked to the administrator like the optimal choice may have appeared paternalistic to the community.

Changes in the Communities

The efforts by Cincinnati's administrators might have failed had not a parallel process been underway in the communities. Comments from community leaders suggest three lessons they had to learn before community involvement could proceed smoothly:

1. They had to learn how to demonstrate the legitimacy of their groups. Several leaders talked about a need to demonstrate to city hall both their numerical support in the community and their personal knowledge of community needs.

2. They had to learn where to go and what to ask for in city hall. Municipal governments are complex organizations that can

be difficult to access. As one community leader said, "There is a game. If you're going to be successful, you learn where the pressure points are, who to talk to, how to get things done" (p. 100).

3. They needed to learn how to lobby and negotiate. As one leader noted, "One of the steps in the process is to actually go lobby with the departments." Once there, they had to be willing to negotiate. As another community representative said, "If you're constantly on the offensive, they [department officials] back up and keep backing away from you" (p. 100).

All of this took time. Both the administrators and the community leaders talked about a learning process that extended over a period of years. For those willing, however, the results appeared to prove worth the time spent.

———————◆———————

Managers must also know how to assert quality standards that they believe must be respected. It can be tempting to succumb to the view that, as one Cincinnati division head said of his response to community demands, "If it's legal, we're probably going to do it." Managers must not lose sight of their legitimate preferences; in negotiations, both sides assert interests.

At the same time, managers should remain open to legitimate public questioning of the standards. That questioning can reveal errors in the standards, as when challenges from the public forced Forest Service negotiators to reexamine their assumptions about scientific standards (Manring, 1993, p. 349). Those negotiators came to recognize that some of the supposed standards were unsupported conventional wisdom. Instead of undermining scientific standards, challenges from citizen group representatives forced the Forest Service "to have a firm scientific basis for all of its decisions."

In short, public managers need many skills to work effectively with the public. Managers must be able to listen well, to change their thinking in response to what they hear, but also to hold fast on important technical or scientific standards. This calls for a balancing act that may, in turn, require a long adjustment process. It is time well spent, however, if it determines whether public involvement brings more benefits than costs.

Should Citizen Groups Be Assisted?

Government is sometimes asked to assist citizen groups. Requests have focused principally on directly funding the building of the organizational capacities of the groups, or, as a more limited option, helping the groups to develop better information on issues.

The rationale for such assistance is clear. Citizen groups enter public involvement at a disadvantage relative to governmental agencies, public managers, and traditional interest groups. The frequent reliance on volunteers limits the time citizen groups can give to a process of involvement, and tight budgets and limited expertise limit their ability to engage effectively in debates of complex issues. In Food and Drug Administration regulatory deliberations, for example, consumer advocates have complained that "consumer organizations have neither manpower nor resources to support their representatives and provide them with the knowledge base available to industry" (Friedman, 1978, p. 212). These problems are especially acute early in public involvement when citizen groups are also building their relationship with government.

Nonetheless, governmental agencies should still be cautious about directly assisting citizen groups. To begin with, involving the public is a labor-intensive process that could require the hiring of either additional staff or private consultants in order to, for instance, obtain the group facilitation skills necessary for running public meetings. Agencies should consider these potential internal resource needs before allocating assistance to citizen groups. However, even if surplus funds are available, financing special assistance to citizen groups may still not be advisable. Such assistance can be counterproductive, doing more harm than good to citizen groups and to the process of public involvement.

Organizational Subsidies

Consider first the possibility of special subsidies to assist in developing citizen groups, an option first attempted on a large scale in the 1960s with the federal War on Poverty, which targeted substantial funding to the building of community organizations in low-income areas. Funds went both to underwrite the formation and operation of organizations and to pay residents for attending meetings. The intent was to build community organizations where none had existed, with the idea that those organizations would in turn help to rebuild their home communities.

The results were mixed, at best. First, the subsidies often distorted who became involved and what they advocated. The availability of governmental subsidies sometimes attracted participants more interested in benefiting from the subsidies than in advocating for broader citizen interests. Some subsidies evolved into patronage attenuated from the original purpose of organizing communities.

Over the long term, subsidies also compromised the ability of many community organizations to advocate for their communities. As Gittell and her associates (1980, pp. 64–65) have argued, subsidies mean higher "external dependence" by these organizations, and "advocacy strategies require an independence of action not readily compatible with external dependence." The result may be an evolution of these organizations "from advocacy to service," from initially fighting for neighborhood interests to eventually functioning only as a service arm of government (p. 40).

Government should not necessarily disdain all assistance for citizen groups. Outside assistance can be an important means for correcting the elitist tendencies of public involvement, as documented in Cincinnati: "Whatever the shortcomings of the [War on Poverty] effort in terms of mobilizing people, it is clear that had the effort not been made, the neighborhood movement in Cincinnati would have an even more pronounced socioeconomic bias than is already the case" (Thomas, 1986, p. 70).

The best strategy, if financial assistance is possible, may be to provide modest grants that are available only for community mobilization and awarded only in response to proposals. These conditions should eliminate claimants who are only interested in the money, narrowing the competition to those who are interested primarily in their communities. Many American cities have developed programs along these lines with evident success (see Hallman, 1984, p. 151).

Technical Assistance

Another option for government in working with citizen groups is to assist these groups in understanding information on important public issues. This assistance can be justified in part on the grounds of equity: resource-poor citizen groups may be unable on their own to develop the understanding necessary to compete with traditional interest groups, especially those representing commercial concerns. Governmental agencies may also benefit from this assistance since, without good information and a good understanding of technical issues, citizen groups may pose more of a threat to governmental quality requirements.

In that spirit, since the 1970s many governmental agencies have allocated funds to support technical assistance for citizen groups. In a recent example at the federal level, the Superfund Amendments and Reauthorization Act of 1986 included grants for technical assistance on cleanup projects (Chess, Long, and Sandman, 1990). At the local level, New York City funds professional consultants for citizen advisory committees (CACs) involved with environmental issues (see Cohen, 1995).

As with organizational subsidies, the wisdom of providing technical assistance is also questionable. In the first place, institutionalizing citizen group advisers within government creates positions with divided loyalties. Advisers may be charged with assisting citizen groups, yet report to public managers who do not see eye-to-eye with those groups. That can create a role conflict for the adviser, as happened with early community planners (see Needleman and Needleman, 1974, pp. 315–316).

Second, this assistance "may exacerbate, not lessen, public opposition to an agency's proposal," as the New York City experience illustrates (Cohen, 1995, p. 125). Technical assistance to CACs there raised new concerns among citizens, but has not facilitated dispute resolution.

These problems may say less about the value of technical assistance *per se* than about the importance of the context in which assistance is provided. The CACs in New York City too often were asked to "react to proposals already formalized by the City," rather than being involved early in decision making. As Cohen (1995, p. 131) notes, "If the CAC's ability to get alternatives adopted is circumscribed by being formed late in the game, the CAC's consultant will be relegated to the less helpful role of merely reviewing and commenting on the City's plans."

In short, technical assistance cannot atone for other sins in public involvement. It can help in resolving issues only if it is part of a public involvement that heeds the other guidelines for effective involvement.

A Long-Term Strategy

An important implication for a long-term strategy for assuring effective public involvement is that, although government may choose to provide direct assistance to citizen groups, the most important assistance remains a well-planned and appropriately structured process of public involvement. A crucial element in this process is influence over substantial public resources. As Berry, Portney, and

Thomson (1993, p. 295) argue based on their analysis of the participation of neighborhood groups in municipal governance, "they must have authority to allocate some significant goods and services in their communities. This means that powers must be taken away from the agencies at city hall that currently exercise such authority and transferred unequivocally to neighborhood organizations." Only this authority can hold the interest and nurture the vitality of citizen groups over the long term.

Chapter Nine

New Forms of Public Involvement

As citizens and public managers build productive relationships, public involvement can evolve in directions beyond the basic forms described in Chapters Seven and Eight. This chapter examines five advanced forms of public involvement: (1) ombudspersons and action centers, (2) coproduction, (3) volunteerism, (4) institutionalized citizen roles in decision making, and (5) structures for protecting the public interest. The first three forms represent advanced citizen roles in service delivery; the latter two represent advanced involvement in decision making. All five can prove useful to government and public managers as well as to citizens and citizen groups.

Ombudspersons and Action Centers

Citizens experience many problems with the delivery of governmental services: trash is not collected, a Social Security check is not received, a pothole is not filled, and so on. As with the products and services of private businesses, such problems are inevitable.

Also inevitably, many citizens contact government to seek solutions to these problems. How government responds to such contacts—Does the agency resolve the complaint? Is the agency's response prompt and courteous?—can affect the quality of life for citizens, while at the same time shaping how citizens feel about government generally.

The evidence indicates that American government usually performs well on these scores. According to national polls, citizens who have made requests of the governmental bureaucracy report high levels of satisfaction—substantially higher than in other nations— with how the requests were treated (Goodsell, 1983, pp. 24–29, 56–58). Yet governmental agencies are not always responsive, and citizens confronted with the complexity of government are also often puzzled about where to take their complaints. To address both problems, many governments have established institutionalized complaint mechanisms to assist citizens in finding solutions for their problems with government. The principal mechanisms are ombudspersons and action centers.

Ombudspersons

An ombudsperson, an innovation borrowed from Scandinavia, serves as a neutral third party employed by government to assist citizens in obtaining responses to their requests or complaints about governmental agencies and, sometimes, private businesses. By virtue of their independence, ombudspersons can work to resolve complaints without fear of incurring the wrath of the affected agencies.

Ombudspersons have been used at the state level, for example. After experiments in a number of states during the middle 1970s, Congress in 1978 passed legislation "requiring every state to have a long-term health care ombudsman program" (Gormley, 1986, p. 187). These ombudspersons work to resolve complaints "from nursing home residents, family members, and other interested parties" on such subjects as "Medicaid programs, guardianship, the power of attorney, inadequate hygiene, family problems, and theft of personal items."

Action Centers

Action centers function similarly, and can even be described as administrative ombudsperson offices. One difference, however, is that the charter of action centers seldom extends to complaints about private businesses. Action centers are especially common at the local level, where, according to a recent survey, almost two-thirds of U.S. cities with populations of at least one hundred thousand have action centers (Scavio, 1993, p. 99).

Sharp (1990, pp. 85–86) has described how a typical action center in Kansas City, Missouri, operates:

> The unit handles complaints and requests concerning virtually any city service except for policing, for which there is a separate complaints process. When a complaint or request is received, the Action Center opens a case file on it and refers the problem to the appropriate city department, thus providing a clearinghouse function for citizens who do not know their way through the city bureaucracy. The Action Center also keeps track of departmental responses to each problem, and keeps citizens informed of the status of their requests. When a department reports completion of response to a problem, the Action Center sends the citizen a postcard requesting an evaluation of the department's response. The Action Center follows up on any case in which the evaluation card is returned with a poor rating.

The evidence suggests that both ombudspersons and action centers can be effective in resolving citizen complaints. The state long-term health care ombudsperson offices reported having resolved more than 85 percent of the complaints they received in one recent year (Gormley, 1986, p. 187). Sharp's evaluation of the Kansas City Action Center suggested positive outcomes there, too.

More important, these mechanisms may produce better outcomes for citizens than taking complaints either to elected officials or directly to departments. As Sharp (1986, pp. 116–118) has observed, administrators may balk at requests from elected officials, viewing those requests as political interference. Direct requests of departments may also meet with resistance. Action centers and ombudspersons, by contrast, have both bureaucratic legitimacy and authority sufficient to persuade agencies to respond.

Tracking complaints that come through complaint mechanisms can also provide valuable information about more general problems with agency operations or about the quality of agency management (see Sharp, 1990, p. 86). Illustrative of this potential, Scavio (1993, p. 99) found that 58 percent of cities with populations of more than one hundred thousand that have ombudspersons or action offices "use the information gathered by these officials for feedback purposes."

Coproduction

Rather than being only the receiver of governmental services, citizens and citizen groups sometimes combine with government in joint production, or coproduction, of services. In these ventures, both citizens and government agents shape the nature and outcomes of services.

Coproduction became the subject of extensive scholarly commentary during the 1980s (see Levine, 1984; Brudney and England, 1983; Whitaker, 1980). In part, that commentary reflects the same reconceptualization of governmental services that underlies public involvement in general. In contrast to the traditional view of service delivery as a hierarchical, top-down process, many services are now viewed as requiring mutual adjustment with an actively participating public. In these services, as Whitaker (1980, p. 240) explained, "only the individual served can accomplish the change. He or she is a vital 'coproducer' of any personal transformation that occurs. The agent can supply encouragements, suggest options, illustrate techniques, and provide guidance and advice, but the agent alone cannot bring about the change. Rather than an agent presenting a 'finished product' to the citizens, agent and citizen together produce the desired transformation."

This commentary also reflects, in part, a growth of coproduction as a by-product of the expansion of other forms of public involvement. As Brudney and England (1983, p. 60) noted, "the coproduction model is based on the assumption of an active, participative populace" with many "consumer producers." Public involvement has helped to increase the number of active consumer producers.

Although it affects all levels of government, coproduction is most common at the local level, where the two classic examples of coproduction are found. The first is education, a service that recognizes the "importance of parents' actions in the education of their children." The other is crime prevention, which is now viewed as unlikely to be effective unless citizens assist (see Whitaker, 1980, p. 243).

Forms of Coproduction

Coproduction comes in a variety of forms. It can involve only individual citizens, such as when a person takes garbage to the curb for municipal pickup; or it may involve citizen groups working as organizations, such as when a neighborhood organization assists in running a recreation center.

Individual-level coproduction has drawn the most attention in the area of crime prevention. Based on citizen surveys in four metropolitan areas, Percy (1987, pp. 84–85) has documented how individual citizens join to coproduce "safety and security" by putting extra locks on doors, placing identification markings on property, purchasing watchdogs, buying light-timing devices, and the like.

There are varieties of coproduction at the group level, too. In perhaps the simplest form, neighborhood groups assist in the monitoring of municipal programs and services, providing another mechanism for reporting problems to municipal officials, who are expected to modify services as their part of the coproduction. Here, too, the best-known examples are in crime prevention; most large cities now sponsor neighborhood block-watch programs using organized citizen groups to observe and report crimes and other suspicious activities (Scavio, 1993, p. 102).

Involvement of citizen groups in service delivery becomes more substantial when, in a second form of coproduction, they supplement a city's supply of unskilled labor for occasional cleanup and maintenance. This involvement often takes the form of short-term cleanup campaigns, as when a neighborhood group asks residents to assist in cleaning up their neighborhood on a given weekend. Municipal efforts of this kind are common in parks, highway maintenance, and waste collection services.

In the most advanced form of coproduction, citizen groups assume significant program operation responsibilities, sometimes even administering particular services, though usually with governmental assistance. This cooperation remains coproduction, rather than strict contracting, as long as the groups volunteer time beyond that for which they are directly reimbursed by government.

Research in Cincinnati revealed several versions of this form of coproduction (Thomas, 1987). In one version, several neighborhood organizations assumed day-to-day responsibility for running recreation centers after the city's recreation department indicated that it could afford to build but not to staff more centers. In a second version, neighborhood organizations assisted in administering community health clinics on contracts with the health department. In a third, community development corporations (CDCs) rehabilitated buildings, usually residences, with the aid of grants or low-interest loans from the city. A municipal housing division official described the CDCs "as an extension of our staff" (Thomas, 1987, p. 100), much as proponents of coproduction have envisioned. The CDCs eventually sold rehabilitated houses on the private market, recycling profits into more rehabilitation.

Benefits and Limits of Coproduction

Coproduction is advertised as bringing many benefits. According to Levine (1984), "The strategy of coproduction promises to be a powerful tool for resolving fiscal stress and an auspicious start on the road to restoring the trust and support of citizens for their public institutions."

Reality has not matched this rhetoric, but coproduction still holds promise for public managers and citizens. In Cincinnati, for example, municipal administrators reported a number of gains from their involvement in coproduction. Service monitoring and unskilled labor were seen as increasing service levels without requiring additional governmental resources. Neighborhood involvement in program operation was viewed as adding to governmental productivity because neighborhood groups volunteered time in addition to what the government paid for.

Individual-level coproduction can bring comparable benefits. Crime can be reduced by "hardening-the-target" initiatives that make homes more difficult to break into (Percy, 1987). Municipal capacities for waste collection and recycling can be enhanced by persuading citizens to bring their waste to the curb and to sort recyclables. Coproduction can also increase governmental efficiency if more services can be provided for the same cost; and costs could decline if coproduction allows government to cut spending.

At the same time, there are limits to these benefits. To begin with, coproduction is usually confined to areas in which minimal expertise is required, both because municipal professionals resist citizen intrusions on their professional prerogatives and because citizens usually lack expertise that they are able and willing to contribute to providing services. As Percy (1987, p. 90) has argued on crime prevention, "citizens are not trained as professional crime fighters, nor do they treat their coproductive involvement as a full-time occupation."

Coproduction is also limited by being more common in areas in which government need not depend on it, such as with maintenance that might otherwise be postponed or cleanups that departments could have managed unassisted. As documented in one survey, program operation by neighborhood groups is usually restricted to "peripheral or supplementary services," as opposed to core public services (Ahlbrandt and Sumka, 1983, p. 218).

This limitation may be encouraged by municipal employees who resist the delegation of essential services to volunteer help because of the threat it poses to their own jobs; or they may object to surrendering essential municipal responsibilities to volunteers who could opt out as easily as they volunteered in. The notorious volatility of neighborhood groups certainly counsels caution about their assumption of important responsibilities.

The financial gains to government from coproduction may also be mostly illusory. Contrary to some claims, contributions from citizens or citizen groups seldom permit cutbacks in governmental budgets. In Percy's (1987, p. 90) words, "The value of citizen coproduction is as an effective complement" to governmental efforts, not as a substitution for those efforts. In addition, coproduction can bring new costs, since government often must provide financial incentives to spur an expanded citizen role. In the Cincinnati case, neighborhood involvement in substantial and reliable coproduction usually developed only when government offered subsidies (Thomas, 1987). Otherwise, faced with new service needs, neighborhoods would, as one of their leaders said, "try to get an agency in the community to provide those services or get the city to do it" (p. 102). There are also costs to developing and monitoring coproduction arrangements, since they cannot run themselves.

Pursuing Coproduction

With these limitations, coproduction still holds enough potential to recommend its pursuit by public managers. That pursuit requires a complex approach as part of a broader public involvement strategy.

First, managers need to be aware of the potential for coproduction, and ensure that other staff are also aware. As Whitaker (1980,

p. 246) has argued, "service agencies need to encourage agents to develop and use their own good judgment and share service responsibility with clients." That awareness "is especially important for services which seek transformation of the behavior of the person being served."

Second, managers should recognize that much coproduction is premised on an advanced level of public involvement. Only relatively advanced public involvement can build the mutual trust necessary for citizen groups and public managers to collaborate in the manner coproduction requires. Without that trust, citizen groups may question the motives of governmental officials, who may in turn question the capacity of the citizen groups.

Third, although it often evolves from other kinds of public involvement, coproduction still requires advance planning. Managers should consider where citizens or citizen groups could assist, as well as what responsibilities might interest those groups. With advanced forms of coproduction, the manager may also need to articulate contractual arrangements with coproducing entities.

Fourth, when coproduction is desired, government should consider what incentives can be offered to gain citizen assistance. Offering influence to citizens in the planning of the service is a prerequisite, but a direct financial subsidy may also be required.

Volunteerism

Citizens may also get involved as volunteers who donate their time to assist in providing public services. Although coproduction often finds citizens giving their time in this manner, volunteerism here refers only to efforts "in which those donating time and labor to public agencies are not the primary beneficiaries of the goods and/or services they help to create" (Brudney, 1990, p. 17).

Talk of volunteerism brings to mind the nonprofit sector, but volunteers also figure prominently in the delivery of government services. According to a 1985 survey, unpaid volunteers were used by almost three-fourths of a broad cross section of U.S. cities ranging from 4,500 to more than 200,000 in population (Duncombe, 1985).

Governmental use of volunteers may have expanded recently. A growing elderly population provides a larger pool from which to recruit, and the maturing of public involvement may have nurtured more volunteering by producing "a gradual warming in adversarial relationships between public administrators and citizens" (Brudney, 1990, p. 13). The forms volunteerism takes are too numerous to detail fully. Volunteers serve in governmental roles ranging from firefighters to senior citizen center assistants to library aides (Duncombe, 1985, p. 360).

The use of volunteers promises many of the gains possible with coproduction, especially increased service levels at little additional cost to government. Volunteers can deliver high-quality services, and their dedication can bring a special spirit to the agencies where they work (Brudney, 1990, pp. 56–59, 66). In addition, as with other forms of public involvement, a well-planned volunteer initiative can build support for the programs in which the volunteers work.

To achieve those gains, managers must carefully plan and structure volunteer programs. This means considering the positions in which volunteers could help, being certain that those positions complement rather than compete with regular paid staff, and selecting volunteers whose skills fit the positions.

The most common problem for volunteer programs is "getting enough people to volunteer" (Duncombe, 1985, p. 362), a problem that can be especially acute for governments, given the many opportunities for volunteers in the nonprofit sector. Solving the problem may require development of a recruitment plan targeting likely locations of prospects. Recruitment can also be enhanced by other public involvement efforts that bring potential volunteers into contact with programs in which volunteers are desired.

Once recruited and placed, volunteers usually need training on agency goals and procedures to ensure compliance with both. Supervision is also necessary, but, "given the relative autonomy of volunteers, a heavy-handed approach to supervision can be expected to elicit antagonism and attrition, rather than compliance" (Brudney, 1990, p. 109). The better approaches entail "persuasion, negotiation, coaching, and teamwork," the same tactics useful in other forms of public involvement.

These various needs may impose costs on government. Someone must plan the programs, select and recruit appropriate volunteers, arrange for training, and perform other tasks that arise. As a consequence, managers should consider in advance the likely costs and benefits before launching a volunteer program.

Institutionalized Roles in Decision Making

There is no better way to ensure the long-term success of public involvement than to institutionalize a decision-making role for that involvement. Regular opportunities to exert influence over substantial resources serve to motivate citizens and citizen groups to remain active.

Municipal governments have experimented with a variety of these institutionalized roles. In some of the earliest experiments at the height of federal urban spending in the 1970s, cities created influential roles for citizen groups in the allocation of federal Community Development Block Grant (CDBG) funds (for a survey, see Dommel, 1982). Officials in Carbondale, Illinois, for example, vested principal CDBG decision-making authority in a Community Development Citizens Steering Committee comprised of a representative sample of city residents (Jackson, 1982).

Some cities have gone a step further to accord citizens a substantial role in determining how municipal revenues will be spent. In some cases, neighborhoods participate in allocating municipal capital improvement budgets. Neighborhood groups in Birmingham, Alabama, for instance, have full authority over these funds (Berry, Portney, and Thomson, 1993, p. 65): "Each neighborhood receives an allocation of capital funds coming into the city, governed by a strict formula based on population and income level. . . . The neighborhood, through its elected officers and its open meetings, determines how those funds will be spent. . . . This system has handled a great deal of funding, sometimes on the order of hundreds of thousands of dollars for a neighborhood with a few thousand people."

Elsewhere, neighborhood groups have been assigned roles in planning basic municipal budgets. In cities such as St. Paul, Cincinnati, and Dayton, neighborhoods define their needs as the first step in the budget process. Requests are then channeled to the appropriate city departments for consideration in the development of departmental requests (Hallman, 1984, pp. 245–246).

More common at all levels of government may be sharing of authority over governmental decisions that do not offer direct dollar benefits to participating groups. These roles range from neighborhood participation in reviewing local zoning requests (Hallman, 1984, pp. 244–245) to participation by consumer representatives in reviewing proposed new drugs (Friedman, 1978). Although they lack the compelling incentive of substantial dollar resources, these regularized opportunities for influence over important decisions also help to sustain citizen interest.

Structures for Protecting the Public Interest

Increased public involvement brings a risk that, in trying to satisfy the many private interest groups who become involved, the broader public interest may be neglected. Critics have argued that increased citizen participation encourages a proliferation of new interest groups, sometimes resulting in "hyperpluralism" (see Lineberry, 1983, pp. 54–60), a brand of politics in which numerous private interest groups dominate public decisions. At the local level, interest groups made so many demands in the 1970s that some harried municipal officials supposedly lost sight of the broader public interest (see Bell and Held, 1969; Yates, 1977).

Research suggests that these concerns may be exaggerated. As Berry, Portney, and Thomson (1993, p. 185) concluded on the role of neighborhood groups: "Yes, the neighborhood organizations do promote the interests of their neighborhood as their top priority. But, no, that promotion of neighborhood interests is not unhealthy. Instead, our respondents tended to agree, it provides a healthy balance to a political system that might otherwise be excessively focused on development of the central business district." Still, public involvement should not be pursued without recognition of the need to protect the public interest. What may be required, in particular, is the creation of special public involvement forums designed to define the public interest, in general or on specific issues, and to articulate means for its achievement.

These forums should represent key citizen groups, including private or narrow geographical interests such as neighborhoods as well as broader interests. The public interest cannot be protected by attempting to shield its shaping and pursuit from the influence of powerful citizen groups. Government officials, including public managers, should then use forums like any other public involvement gathering, sharing concerns about the public interest as well as any information that corroborates concerns.

Governments at all levels have experimented with these forums in recent years. At the local level, many communities have initiated "community goal-setting" efforts "directed towards identifying desired ends and developing the means to achieve those ends" (Vogel and Swanson, 1988, p. 44). Although these efforts predate the new public involvement, earlier initiatives usually involved only community elites, whereas contemporary community goal setting encourages extensive involvement through a combination of citizen surveys, public meetings, mass media discussions and advertising, and even unofficial referenda (see for example, McClendon and Lewis, 1985; Vogel and Swanson, 1988; McGuire, Rubin, Agranoff, and Richards, 1994).

Communitywide strategic planning has emerged recently as the most popular community goal-setting strategy. Common in private business circles for some years, strategic planning now enjoys popularity in all manner of organizations. At the municipal level, this planning differs from other goal-setting approaches by its use of environmental scanning for defining constraints and opportunities and by its concern with seeing that recommendations are implemented (Vogel and Swanson, 1988, p. 47). This planning also usually features extensive public involvement.

This planning may increase public involvement over the long term as well as the short term. Analysts (McGuire, Rubin, Agranoff, and Richards, 1994, p. 431) of a recent matched-group study of strategic planning and control communities concluded that "a communitywide strategic planning process improves the political climate of a community. The process of gathering input from residents, discussing the community's weaknesses, working toward consensus, and implementing projects through teams makes a significant difference in the way a community addresses important issues." The researchers also found that this planning enhanced the overall development of the communities.

Communities have also tailored their own structures for promoting the public interest. Supporters of a school tax levy in Cincinnati conceived a strategy to focus the levy campaign on neighborhoods, hoping to mobilize those many narrow geographic interests behind a citywide concern. The need for a levy was explained to neighborhood organizations in a series of meetings held *before* the size of the levy was specified, such that the eventual size could reflect neighborhood input, and neighborhoods were asked at the same time to play a primary role in the campaign. The result was a referendum victory by a 55 percent majority, a sharp contrast to a two-to-one ratio of defeat for a similar proposal launched without neighborhood support a year earlier. By structuring public involvement to encourage neighborhood attention to schools, levy supporters were able to utilize neighborhood groups to promote that citywide interest (Thomas, 1986, pp. 147–148). Similar strategies for other jurisdiction-wide issues have succeeded elsewhere.

Some recent regional partnership efforts reflect a similar approach. In these efforts, business, government, universities, and nonprofit agencies come together, usually with the aid of public involvement, to address jurisdiction-wide issues. When the federal environmental role declined in the 1980s, for example, state and local actors united to address environmental issues from the bottom up in the so-called "civic environmentalism" movement (John, 1994): "The key was the emergence of a 'shadow community' of environmental professionals in agencies, business, and environmental groups who created a local collaborative process, cutting across the fragmented system established by federal statutes. The shadow community developed a shared understanding of practical steps that could be taken to solve local problems."

None of these mechanisms provides a foolproof strategy, but together they offer a menu of options for protecting the public interest from private assaults. The public interest need not and should not be a casualty of increased public involvement.

Chapter Ten

Public Involvement and the Effective Public Manager

The need to work with the active involvement of the public provides opportunities for managers to increase their effectiveness and the effectiveness and legitimacy of government. This chapter offers concluding recommendations for how public managers can make the best use of these opportunities.

The recommendations are offered at two levels. At the operational level, the first part of this chapter summarizes the most important lessons of the preceding chapters, presenting a set of recommendations on how public managers should—and should not—work with public involvement. At a more abstract level, the second part of the chapter examines how the new involvement should be seen as part of a broader transformation of public management that calls for the development of new managerial skills. Returning to the larger questions of effectiveness and legitimacy with which this book began, a final section considers the benefits these new skills can bring to public managers and to the work of democratic governance.

Dos and Don'ts

Achieving effective public involvement can be a painstaking process requiring much attention to detail. Nonetheless, public managers can make a good start toward successful involvement by keeping in mind a short list of "dos and don'ts."

1. *Anticipate issues rather than let them be imposed from elsewhere.* A first step toward resolving any issue is to anticipate it before it is

imposed. As reported in Chapter Three, issues initiated by managers are more likely to be resolved successfully than issues that are forced upon them. Issues that originate elsewhere usually carry more constraints by the time they reach the manager.

This recommendation is not necessarily linked to public involvement, since the manager should initiate issues before deciding if and how to involve the public. Issues are more readily anticipated, however, if the manager keeps a finger on the public pulse, such as by maintaining ongoing contacts with the public. These contacts could be part of "management by wandering around," the tactic of pursuing regular informal contacts with clients and employees that successful managers supposedly use to stay in touch with their organizations (see Peters and Waterman, 1982, p. 122; Behn, 1991, pp. 136–137).

2. *Define issues in terms more amenable to resolution.* Whenever an issue is identified, the manager should attempt to define the issue in terms that will facilitate resolution. This means, for one thing, avoiding definition of the issue in the either-or terms that are so resistant to compromise, as with many "not in my backyard" issues. The manager should also attempt to minimize the levels of government to be involved, since issues that can be limited fairly to one governmental level stand the best chance of reaching a successful outcome.

There are limits to what managers can do here. From an ethical perspective, a manager should not exclude any governmental unit that has a legitimate stake in an issue, and many issues inherently hold the interest of two or more levels of government. From a practical perspective, a manager may be unable to "unstructure" an issue that arose as a structured choice. Managers should endeavor only to avoid unnecessary constraints and complications.

3. *Do not view public involvement as good or bad per se.* The scholarly literature tilts heavily in favor of public involvement, often implying that participation will improve any decision. The reactions of practitioners tilt the other way, suggesting that public

involvement is an unwelcome intrusion on the managerial prerogatives. The wise manager will avoid taking either perspective.

The questions of whether and how to involve the public are better viewed as issue specific, because some issues are better resolved with public involvement, and other issues without. To be sure, the latter issues are not as common as the history of public management suggests. Seen in this light, the scholarly bias in favor of public involvement in part reflects recognition that managers have involved the public less than they should have.

Even when recommended by the substance of an issue, inviting public involvement will not inevitably lead to a better outcome. Whether that involvement succeeds or fails depends on managers knowing how to invite and facilitate the effort. Poorly planned involvement can be as hazardous as excluding the public, even if involvement appears essential. Conversely, well-planned involvement should enhance the chances of resolving the issue and implementing the resolution.

4. *Know what you want from public involvement.* In many of the cases examined in this book, public managers invited public involvement without first defining what they wanted from involvement. When that happens, managers are unlikely to get what they *need* from public involvement, and they may get surprises they neither need nor want, such as antagonism from the public and threats to important scientific or technical standards.

Public involvement offers two principal benefits for public managers: (1) more information on public preferences, on the effectiveness of existing programs, or on other aspects of issues; and (2) public acceptance of decisions as a prerequisite to implementation of those decisions. Before inviting involvement, managers should have considered which of these benefits are desired.

5. *Recognize that public involvement requires a sharing of decision-making authority.* As a rule, participation of the public should not be invited unless the manager will share this authority. Since citizens may reasonably expect that their opinions will influence the

eventual decision, failure to grant that influence risks alienating the public or even arousing their opposition.

With some forms of involvement, the manager need not relinquish much authority. Citizen surveys, for example, ask so small a contribution of citizens' time that no authority need be surrendered. Even a survey makes no sense, however, unless the manager will at least consider citizen opinions. To do otherwise is to waste everyone's time.

6. *Define in advance what can and cannot be negotiated.* Sharing of authority does not mean that all aspects of the issue must be open to public scrutiny. On the contrary, all public decisions come with quality requirements, that is, scientific, technical, or budgetary constraints on what can be done or how much money can be spent. The public manager is obligated to specify in advance what these constraints are.

While recognizing this fact, public managers have often failed to define their quality requirements *before* public involvement is initiated; yet waiting until later can result in citizens' feeling misled about their role, perhaps undermining the viability of the entire involvement process.

Difficulties arise because quality requirements are not always obvious. The line between a personal preference and a quality requirement is often blurred. To cope with these difficulties, managers should attempt to define their quality requirements early on, but remain open to the possibility that public involvement will reveal a need to reconsider.

7. *Define in advance what segments of the public should be involved.* Once a need for involvement is evident, the manager must try to define what segments of the public, including both organized and unorganized groups, can satisfy that need. This effort, too, should be made before public involvement is invited, since the form of the invitation depends in part on whose participation is desired.

A poor definition carries serious risks. Focusing on too broad a public can unnecessarily complicate decision making, while overlooking an important group risks later failure if that group mobilizes around the issue. This latter risk should be the greater concern to managers in the early stages of decision making. It will usually be more difficult to accommodate later the demands of a group that was mistakenly excluded than to tolerate the apathy of an uninterested group that was mistakenly included.

As with other aspects of public involvement, the initial definition of the public should not be viewed as final. Regardless of how much care is taken at the outset, overlooked publics may eventually appear on the scene demanding a role. Managers must be open to those requests.

8. *Whenever a need for acceptance requiring involvement is identified, consider citizen attitudes toward organizational goals.* The vast majority of the public involvement cases examined in this book brought a need for public acceptance that could not be assumed unless the public were involved. This is probably true for a substantial majority of public management issues. Whenever this need is evident, the manager should consider how citizens may feel about the agency's goals.

If citizens are likely to agree with the goals, the manager should maximize public involvement, inviting them to be an equal partner in decision making. With so much need for acceptance and so little threat to agency goals, the manager should decide jointly with the public through a public decision approach.

If citizens instead disagree with agency goals, the manager should invite public involvement with less sharing of authority. That can be achieved through consultation, in which the manager consults with the public and gives weight to its opinions, but retains final authority for making the decision. Managers can choose between unitary consultation, in which the public is involved as a single group, and segmented consultation, in which different segments of the public are involved at different times or in different arenas. Which is preferable depends on whether the problem is structured, with choice restricted to predefined alternatives, and whether there is significant conflict within the public over the preferred solution (see also Chapter Five).

9. *Select the appropriate decision-making form.* Once the decision-making approach has been selected, the manager must select the appropriate form of involvement. Selection among many options, including citizen surveys, key contacts, public meetings, advisory committees, and mediation, should be based on a combination of the decision-making approach and the nature of the relevant public.

More often than not, managers are best advised to use more than one form of involvement. For example, a manager might choose initially to conduct a citizen survey to obtain basic information on the issue, and later establish an advisory committee or hold a series of public meetings to engage more substantial involvement.

10. *Work to build the relationship.* Taking the right approach in the appropriate forum will go a long way toward achieving successful public involvement, but the manager must also work within that context to build a good working relationship with the public (Fisher and Brown, 1988). Knowing how to communicate with the public is part of the task, and that communication must be two-way: the manager must listen closely to the public as well as articulate clearly the agency's perspective. Managers must also recognize any needs for education, both structured education, such as special presentations by agency experts, and informal learning, which occurs as the two sides work together.

11. *Keep an eye on the public interest.* Although public involvement can enhance pursuit of the public interest by involving segments of the public who might otherwise be overlooked, the many publics can also manifest themselves as an array of special interests that do not equal the public interest. Public managers should never become so involved with these many publics that they lose sight of the public interest.

To minimize that risk, the manager should cultivate sources of information in addition to citizens groups. These sources include traditional interest groups, other public administrators, and, most important, the democratically elected superiors to whom public managers are ultimately accountable. Managers can further reduce the threat to the public interest by structuring special forums to encourage its articulation (see also Chapter Nine).

12. *Accept and learn from failure.* No matter how careful the planning or how artful the execution, taking the appropriate approach to public involvement never guarantees success. The problem itself may be intractable, as with efforts to site hazardous waste disposal facilities, in which involvement sometimes leads to adamant opposition to siting at any location.

No approach can succeed with every problem. All a manager can do, if a particular approach fails, is to try to learn from the failure, identifying what might be done differently in the future. Managers appear to have more success anyway when they follow a "ready, fire, aim" strategy, acting or "firing" first, then attempting to refine their "aim" (Peters and Waterman, 1982; Levin and Sanger, 1994).

The Changing Job of the Public Manager

There are grounds for wondering whether public involvement will remain a major concern for public managers. The push for public involvement lost momentum during the 1980s as many elective officials, impatient with the perceived inefficiency of government, showed a renewed reluctance to involve the public in public management. The charge was led by the Reagan administration, which pushed to weaken requirements for public involvement in federal programs. For their part, many public managers, having experienced the disadvantages of public involvement, welcomed the change of heart.

That trend probably represents a temporary change in the political winds rather than any enduring change in the climate of public management. Most of the forces that nurtured a climate favorable to public involvement remain strong:

1. The administrative side of government continues to wield substantial decision-making authority, giving the public ample reason to want to be involved in the managerial process.

2. Rather than disappearing, the citizen groups that were nurtured by the public involvement requirements of the 1960s and 1970s found ways to maintain themselves in the less congenial environment of the 1980s and 1990s, and have even been joined by new citizen claimants on government.

3. The strong participatory bent for which Americans are known seems unlikely to diminish since the higher educational levels that may be the underlying cause continue to increase.

A Changing Environment

The case for the continuing relevance of public involvement also rests on a broader transformation of the work of public management. A variety of forces, including public involvement, has changed the environment of public management, transforming the job of public managers and the skills necessary to perform that job.

The most basic change is that external actors have become much more significant. The expanding role of the federal government in the 1960s and 1970s made federal actors more important to the administration of public programs. The professionalization of state governments during that same period made more prominent actors of state governments, too, such that the administration of all manner of public programs now requires two or more levels of government. Spending cutbacks have not changed this pattern appreciably, because federal and state governments continue to be involved as regulators, if not as principal funders, by mandating standards for programs.

The earlier expansion of federal and state roles also led to more of a role for the nonprofit sector as state and local governments often chose to contract with nonprofit agencies to provide grant-supported services, rather than providing the services directly. Nonprofit agencies came to represent what Don Kettl (1981) termed a "fourth face of federalism."

Declining public sector funding eventually persuaded governmental agencies to give more attention to the private sector as well. If government could not provide services alone or could not provide them effectively, private sector assistance might be enlisted, either on a contract basis or by privatizing services to businesses. Attention to the private sector also grew as state and local governments looked increasingly to economic development as a potential source for new public revenues.

Requirements for increased public involvement contributed to the increased importance of external actors. For reasons both legal and political, public managers were pushed to work with all kinds of publics.

The growing importance of external actors reflects a transition toward what Bryson and Crosby (1992, p. 19) have termed a "shared-power world." In this world, effective action requires cooperation by multiple organizations in the face of a declining "capacity of single organizations, especially governments, to manage and to govern."

Acceptance of a shared-power world destroys any illusion of a politics-administration dichotomy, and in the process undermines the rationale for the traditional insulation of many public managers. As Tipple and Wellman (1991, p. 427) have commented, "Clearly, the 1950s–1960s paradigm of focusing almost exclusively on internal operations geared toward efficiency and economy is inadequate."

Public management has become more permeable, more subject to pressures from outside organizational boundaries.

In a related manner, the work of the public sector has also become less hierarchical. Traditional public and business administration emphasized top-down authority, by which directives flowed downward from the top of the hierarchy to lower-level administrators who were expected to implement the directives. Although it is questionable whether many organizations, public or private, ever followed the hierarchical model closely, the model has become less relevant in recent decades.

The reasons are several. First, the growing importance of actors external to governmental agencies means that managers are working more with people who are outside their formal hierarchical authority. Second, within governmental agencies, employees have balked more at simply following orders from above, asking increasingly for reasons for what they do and a role in deciding what to do. Third, the expanded involvement of government in difficult social problems has increased the discretion available to many so-called "street-level bureaucrats" (Lipsky, 1971), a discretion that is beyond hierarchical control. In short, the idea of a shared-power world applies within government as well as between government and other sectors.

A Need for New Skills

Coping in this new world requires skills that earlier public managers sometimes survived without. To begin with, in a less insular environment, managers must be able to work with a variety of people if agency goals are to be achieved. The increased relevance of external actors demands that managers know how to work with a broader range of people than in the past. The manager must also know how to pull those various people together to reach a decision that can be implemented. In Cleveland's (1975) words, "How do you get everybody in on the act and still get some action?" To do that, managers need the ability to structure appropriate decision-making forums. One-on-one conversations and in-house staff meetings cannot resolve as many issues as they once could.

The manager must be able to shape a decision-making forum appropriate both for the specific issue and for the actors interested in that issue. In matters of public involvement, for example, the manager must be able to choose intelligently between many possible forms of public involvement. The right choice can lead to an effective decision that will be easily implemented; the wrong choice can lead to impasse.

To work effectively within any particular forum, the manager must be able to use facilitation skills to move small and large groups toward consensus, or at least toward decisions that all will accept. Possessing facilitation skills is likely to mean that the manager also knows how to empower others, another of the new talents needed by public managers. Managers must be able to persuade others to join in pursuing common ends and to become leaders themselves in that pursuit. As Bryson and Crosby (1992, p. 55) have argued, "The tasks of leadership in a shared-power world are complex and many. . . . No single person or group can perform them all; that is why leadership must be shared."

Not all public managers can be expected to develop these skills. Managers who are accustomed to working in traditional, relatively insulated managerial roles may be ill-suited to become people-oriented facilitators. Leaders who are, in Fiedler's (1967) terms, "task motivated" may be unable to develop the "relationship-motivated" approach necessary for the new managerial approach described here. The ad hoc nature of this management may also feel foreign to those comfortable working in the same forums with the same actors for many years.

Many managers may feel that they do not have the time to develop these skills, a reasonable objection since other demands on public managers have not diminished. The need for technical expertise has certainly not diminished; public managers must still have the policy knowledge necessary to address the technical requirements for effective public action. That need may even have grown as some problems (for example, environmental issues) have brought even larger technical questions, and as external actors have raised more questions about technical issues. In addition, managers cannot neglect traditional responsibilities for human resources management, budgeting and financial control, and the like.

Still, those managers who cannot develop these new skills would be smart to find means to build the skills elsewhere in their agencies. These skills are demanded by many forces now impinging on public management, not by public involvement alone. Absent these skills, the changing job of the public manager could become impossible.

Public Involvement and Democratic Values

Planned and administered appropriately, public involvement can enhance the effectiveness of public managers and the decisions they make, bringing many gains:

1. Decision quality may improve as citizens and citizen groups add to the information available for making decisions. That information might prevent repetitions of many ill-advised public decisions (for example, high-rise public housing and large-scale residential displacement from urban renewal areas).

2. With citizens involved in making decisions, acceptance of decisions may increase, enhancing the likelihood of successful implementation.

3. If citizens assist in service delivery, services may become more effective and more efficient.

4. As involvement increases citizen understanding of governmental operations, criticism of governmental agencies may lessen, improving the plight of beleaguered bureaucrats.

The most important rewards of public involvement, however, may come in terms of democratic values. We live in an era when the central democratic values of accountability and legitimacy are routinely described as compromised or endangered, with the connections between citizens and their governments said to be badly attenuated. Public involvement, at least as advocated here, could ameliorate this problem. Increased public involvement should enhance accountability by giving citizens new channels through which to communicate with government and to hold government accountable. Greater public involvement should also build the public acceptance of governmental decisions that underlies governmental legitimacy.

Following the recommendations of this book need not risk the "excess of democracy" that Huntington (1975, p. 113) has warned threatens governmental effectiveness if the public becomes too involved in governance. Managers who heed the lessons of this book should not involve the public unnecessarily, and when they do involve the public, they should not permit the public to compromise essential agency quality standards.

Finding the line between too much and too little public participation represents the greatest challenge in public involvement. Just as democracy is not a simple approach to government, so public involvement is not a simple means for bringing democracy to public management. To achieve, at once, effective public involvement, effective public management, and effective democracy, we must find and walk that line. Following the guidelines offered here should help.

Appendix A:
Testing and Refining
the Effective Decision Model

The validity of the Effective Decision Model was tested using data from previously reported cases of possible or actual public involvement. The cases were identified through an extensive survey of the literature in public administration and related fields. Only published cases were considered in an effort to maximize the quality of the case reporting.

The cases also had to qualify as part of "the new public involvement," the movement of the last thirty years. That involvement, including most of the cases in this research, has occurred principally on the administrative side of government. A less common form of the new involvement has occurred as nontraditional policy development (for example, formulation of policy goals for a community by means of surveys and public hearings). A few cases were included in which the public might have been involved but was not. In addition, the theory's decision focus dictated that only cases describing decisions could be considered.

Cases meeting these criteria were screened to assure representation of varieties of public involvement and of the range of substantive areas and the expanse of time in which public involvement has been used. These procedures netted thirty cases for study, or forty-two actual decisions for analysis (nine cases included two or three decisions). The cases are listed at the end of the appendix.

Content analysis was used to code the cases on the quality and acceptability questions, decision effectiveness, and other variables. Operationalizations consisted of the author's narrative explanations of the variables along with the coding options. For example, each of the basic problem characteristics was coded mostly on a dichotomous "yes or no" basis using the explanations provided earlier. The other operationalizations are explained later.

After first reviewing and discussing these operationalizations with the author, a graduate assistant coded each case and provided explanatory notes for each code. The author then independently undertook the same process. When both coders completed work on a case, they met to compare results and to resolve differences with the aid of the case notes. The first few cases required extensive discussion between the coders to refine the variables and codes. In addition, with the cases that included two or three decisions, the coders had to reach agreement on the number and nature of the decisions before coding could be completed.

Across all of the cases, intercoder reliabilities, computed as agreements as a proportion of all codes, totaled .762. Many of the disagreements were minor, however, as the results for the decision effectiveness measures illustrate. Using the earlier listing of its possible elements, effectiveness was coded separately for process and outcome as ineffective (0), mixed or uncertain (1), or effective (2). Agreements as a proportion of all codes totaled .729 for both process and outcome, but gamma statistics of agreement, which give less weight to milder disagreements, reached .892 for process and .983 for outcome. To retain unresolved disagreements, the eventual measures of decision effectiveness were computed as the sum of the two coders' scores.

The structure of the theory also forces attention to cumulative reliabilities. That is, to what extent did the coders agree on all of the problem attributes for each decision, thereby agreeing on the recommended level of involvement? Ignoring cases with either irrelevant disagreements or missing data, this complete intercoder agreement was achieved on 28 of 40 cases (.700).

As Table A.1 shows, the cases capture a diverse public involvement history. Of all the substantive areas, community and economic development receive the most attention, perhaps reflecting greater historical public involvement in these areas. The dates of the cases encompass most of the contemporary experience with new forms of public involvement, except for the slighting of recent experience, which is inevitable in a reanalysis.

The cases strikingly embody the quality-acceptability competition that makes questions of public involvement so difficult. As Table A.2 shows, most of the cases carried quality requirements and required acceptance from a public unlikely to accept an autonomous managerial decision. In addition, the relevant public agreed with agency goals only about a third of the time and disagreed among themselves most of the time. To further complicate matters, those publics usually included both organized and unorganized groups, and a number of other actors were also interested.

Table A.1.   Substantive Focus and Dates of Public Involvement Decisions.

Substantive Focus	Qualifying Cases Percent	(Number)
Community and economic development	21.4 percent	(9)
Housing	9.5 percent	(4)
School desegregation	4.8 percent	(2)
Crime/police	7.1 percent	(3)
Transportation (siting or other planning)	9.5 percent	(4)
Environmental (air, water, parks)	19.0 percent	(8)
Nuclear power	9.5 percent	(4)
Hazardous waste	14.3 percent	(6)
Other	4.8 percent	(2)
TOTAL	99.9 percent	(42)
Date of Decision		
1969–73	31.0 percent	(13)
1975–79	47.6 percent	(20)
1980–84	21.4 percent	(9)
TOTAL	100.0 percent	(42)

Table A.2.   Characteristics of the Public Involvement Decisions.

Characteristic	Qualifying Cases Percentage	(Number)
Problem attributes:		
Quality requirements	92.9 percent	(39)
More information needed	78.6 percent	(33)
Alternative solutions already defined	61.9 percent	(26)
Citizen acceptance needed	85.4 percent	(35)
Acceptance contingent on involvement	90.5 percent	(38)
Citizens share organizational goals	36.6 percent	(15)
Conflict over solutions likely among citizens	70.7 percent	(29)
Interested actors:		
Relevant public of both organized and unorganized groups	64.3 percent	(27)
Two or more levels of government	78.6 percent	(33)
Five or more other actors, in addition to decision maker and citizen groups	54.8 percent	(23)

This complexity probably marks the cases as unlike typical public decisions or public involvement cases, many of which require either no public acceptance or no involvement to assure acceptance and do not interest other actors. This atypicality actually enhances the value of the cases for testing the theory since, if the theory works to any extent with these cases, it could be more powerful with cases in which the quality-acceptability tension is less acute and the burden of complexity less onerous.

Despite this complexity, officials were able to resolve the cases effectively almost half the time. Although the effectiveness of public decisions might appear difficult to assess (see Murray, 1983, pp. 61–62), the many complaints about the unwanted consequences of public involvement imply that the critics believe they can assess this effectiveness. Their criticisms suggest, to begin with, two general dimensions of decision effectiveness. Reflecting the nature of the public sector, effectiveness can be defined in terms of process, how smoothly decision making progresses, and outcome, how well the eventual decision works. Process effectiveness reflects such considerations as (a) level of antagonism or "unpleasantness" (Cupps, 1977, p. 482), (b) the time necessary (Cleveland, 1975), and (c) the ability to reach a decision. Outcome effectiveness encompasses (a) correspondence to quality requirements (were they respected?), (b) success of implementation, (c) citizen or public satisfaction with the eventual decision, (d) managerial satisfaction with the decision, and (e) eventual achievement of the intended goals. As those criteria suggest, decision effectiveness includes both managerial and public perspectives.

If the theory holds, any disparity between recommended and actual public involvement should result in lower decision effectiveness. To test that proposition, the codes for both recommended involvement and actual involvement were converted to numerical scores (that is, A1 = 1, A11 = 3, C1 = 5, C11 = 7, G11 = 9), using two-point intervals to permit coding of a few in-between positions (for example, involvement between C11 and G11 could be coded as 8). A measure of deviation from recommended involvement was then calculated by subtraction as an absolute difference (that is, ignoring whether any deviation was toward more or less involvement than recommended).

As testimony to the value of the Effective Decision Model, across the forty public involvement decisions, this measure of deviation between the actual level of public involvement and the level recommended by the model proved the best statistical predictor of decision effectiveness. As the deviation from the recommended level of involvement *increased*, actual decision effectiveness *decreased* ($r = -.611$).

The data also indicate that managers have most commonly erred by choosing to underinvolve the public. Whereas the median recommended involvement across all of these cases is a unitary public consultation (C11), actual involvement was much lower, with half of the cases using less than a unitary consultation (C1) and almost one-fourth attempting—though not always successfully—to exclude the public entirely. Historically at least, public managers have tended to involve the public much less than appears to be desirable.

It is not involvement by itself that leads to good results. A simple measure of the degree of public involvement is not as strongly associated with higher decision effectiveness ($r = .416$) as is consistency with the recommended level of involvement. As that finding suggests, a manager can involve the public too much. Effective decisions require involving the public to an extent appropriate for the issue at hand.

Nor can any other variable explain decision effectiveness as well as can the measure of the appropriateness of the actual public involvement. As Table A.3 indicates, none of the other variables in the analysis was as strongly associated with decision effectiveness. At the same time, the appropriateness of the public involvement approach is not the only factor useful in explaining decision effectiveness. As Table A.4 shows (and as discussed in earlier chapters), use of stepwise multiple regression analysis identified two additional determinants of overall decision effectiveness:

1. The numbers and competitiveness of levels of government involved in the issue, coded as (1) one level only, (2) two levels—federal and local, (3) two levels—state and local, and (4) three levels—federal, state, and local. ("State and local" was differentiated from "federal and local" because the former appeared to produce more interlevel competition than the latter. There were no two-level, federal-state cases.)

2. Where the issue originated, coded as (1) with the manager, (2) elsewhere in government, or (3) outside of government (that is, with citizens).

Table A.3.   Correlates of Decision Effectiveness.

Predictor	Correlation with Overall Decision Effectiveness
I. Problem attributes	
Additional information needed?	.095
Alternative solutions already defined?	−.315
Citizen acceptance needed?	−.030
Acceptance contingent on involvement?	−.205
Citizens share organization goals?	.331
II. Aspects of involvement	
Deviation of actual from recommended public involvement (absolute)	−.611
Degree of public involvement	.461
Number of involvement mechanisms used	.374
Adequacy of incentives for involvement	.368
III. Contextual characteristics	
Levels of government (number and competitiveness)	−.388
Distance of issue origin from decision maker	−.535
Number of other actors	−.103
Presence of time constraint	−.071
Sufficient resources available for solution	.421
A "NIMBY" issue?	−.454

As Table A.4 shows, combining these two factors with the appropriateness of the actual public involvement can explain more than 60 percent of the variance in the effectiveness of decisions on the cases in the reanalysis.

The initial testing was of the original Vroom-Yetton (1973) model, which was designed for determining how much to involve subordinates, principally in private-sector decisions. Some elements of that model might be inappropriate for issues of public involvement. As a consequence, the model was examined piece by piece to determine which, if any, elements should be modified or excised.

Table A.4.   Explaining Decision Effectiveness:
Multiple Regression Analyses.

Predictor	Zero-Order Correlation	Contribution to Variance Explained
Deviation of actual from recommended public involvement (absolute)	−.611	.373
Levels of government	−.388	.174
Distance of problem origin from decision maker	−.535	.075
TOTAL R²	.622	
ADJUSTED R²	.612	

1. *Quality requirements.* In their original model, the first question Vroom and Yetton (1973, pp. 21–22) asked was whether there are any quality requirements. In the public sector, quality requirements appear to be ubiquitous, such that the question should instead be, What are the quality requirements? Fearing the wrath that can follow even the appearance of malfeasance, policy makers supposedly circumscribe managers' discretion with an "array of laws, procedures, and norms intended to closely control their behavior" (Whorton and Worthley, 1983, p. 126).

The cases in the reanalysis bear out this argument. Only three of the forty cases were initially coded as having no quality requirements, but closer examination suggests that quality requirements may have been present in those cases, too. Moreover, an assumption of quality requirements on all cases improves the fit of the model to the data. With the recommended paths modified to reflect that change, correlations with deviation from the model's recommendations improved from −.571 to the −.611 figure reported earlier.

2. *Acceptance.* Vroom and Yetton also asked two questions about acceptance in their original model: first, whether acceptance is necessary for successful implementation; and second, if accep-

tance is necessary, whether it is reasonably certain if the manager decides alone. Those questions were reduced in the Effective Decision Model to the single two-part fourth question.

Vroom and Yetton appear to have used two separate questions principally to distinguish between structured and unstructured problems in which information is needed and in which acceptance is necessary but reasonably certain if the manager decides alone. When such an issue is structured, Vroom and Yetton recommend the modified autonomous approach; if unstructured, they recommend the group (that is, unitary public) consultation.

With public sector issues, however, the modified autonomous approach appears desirable for the latter situation as well as the former. In contrast to the involvement of subordinates, public participation is too complex and asks too much of both managers and citizens to be desirable in a full consultation if the manager is seeking only information, when acceptance is essentially assured. That being the case, no purpose is served by retaining the acceptance questions as two separate questions in the model.

3. *The relevant public*. Applying the Vroom-Yetton theory to public involvement does raise the issue of how to identify the relevant publics, which can be numerous, diffuse, and much more difficult to define than are the relevant subordinates. This reality was addressed by adding the question about who the relevant public is.

Taken together, these changes greatly simplify the basic Vroom-Yetton model into the Effective Decision Model. Yet that parsimony does not come at any cost in the ability to capture the full range of options necessary for decisions on public issues. In addition, of course, those options can and should be further elaborated by considering the answer to the fifth question (Who is the relevant public?), relative to the discussion of the mechanisms for public involvement in Chapters Six and Seven.

Appendix B:
Public Involvement Cases

Note: Cases are listed by author or, with multiple cases from the same source, by volume editor. Dates refer to year of publication, not case occurrence, and the number of asterisks indicate the number of decisions coded for the case.

Buck, V. J. (1984). The impact of citizen participation programs and policy decisions on participants' opinions. *Western Political Quarterly, 37,* 468–482.*

Cole, R. L. (1983). Participation in community service organizations. *Journal of Community Action, 1,* 53–60.*

From Dommel, P. R., & Associates. (1982). *Decentralizing urban policy: Case studies in community development.* Washington: Brookings Institution.

Hall, J. S. Community Development Block Grant implementation in Phoenix, Arizona, pp. 47–83.**

Haley, L. L. Community Development Block Grant implementation in Allegheny County, Pennsylvania, pp. 166–194.*

Jackson, J. S. Community Development Block Grant implementation in Carbondale, Illinois, pp. 195–222.*

From Ebbin, S., & Kasper, R. (1974). *Citizens groups and the nuclear power controversy: Uses of scientific and technological information.* Cambridge, MA, and London: The MIT Press.

Midland Plant Units 1 and 2, pp. 59–89.*

Vermont Nuclear Power Station, pp. 90–121.**

Rule making hearings: The emergency core cooling system (ECCS), pp. 122–138.*

Ferber, M., & Beard, E. (1980). Marketing urban America: The selling of the Boston Plan and a new direction in federal-urban relations. *Polity, 12,* 539–559.*

Fox, S. F. (1985). Who opposes public/private financial partnerships for urban renewal? A case study. *Journal of Urban Affairs, 7,* 27–40.*

Friedman, R. S. (1978). Representation in regulatory decision making: Scientific, industrial, and consumer inputs to the FDA. *Public Administration Review, 38*, 205–214.*

From Goldman, R. B. (Ed.). (1980). *Roundtable justice: Case studies in conflict resolution*. Boulder, CO: Westview Press.

Gillers, S. New faces in the neighborhood: Mediating the Forest Hills housing dispute, pp. 59–85.**

Fleishman, J. L. Not without honor—A prophet even in his own country: The St. Louis tenant strike of 1969, pp. 87–127.**

Finney, G. S. Desegregating the schools in Dayton, pp. 181–201.*

Harris, I. M. (1980). Community involvement in desegregation: The Milwaukee experience. *Journal of Voluntary Action Research, 9,* 179–188.*

From Howitt, A. M. (1984). *Managing federalism*. Washington: Congressional Quarterly Press.

McCarthy, H. B., & Howitt, A. M. Extending the red line to Arlington, pp. 270–295.*

Howitt, A. M., & Rubin, K. Citizen participation in Oxford, pp. 303–321.*

Kraft, M. E., & Kraut, R. (1985). The impact of citizen participation on hazardous waste policy implementation: The case of Clermont County, Ohio. *Policy Studies Journal, 14,* 170–178.***

Mangione, T. W., & Fowler, F. J (1993). Reducing neighborhood crime: The Hartford experiment. *Journal of Community Action, 1,* 49–53.**

From Mazmanian, D. A., & Nienaber, J. (1979). Can organizations change? Environmental protection, citizen participation, and the Corps of Engineers. Washington, DC: The Brookings Institution.

Project study III: Flood control on Wildcat and San Pablo Creeks: A California showpiece, pp. 103–113.*

Project study V: Flood control on the Middle Fork of the Snoqualmie River, pp. 132–157.***

McClendon, B. W., & Lewis, J. A. (1985). Goals for Corpus Christi: Citizen participation in planning, *National Civic Review, 74,* 72–80.*

Moldenhauer, D. (1986). A case study of victim-centered political action: Jackson Township, New Jersey. In D. Morell & C. Magorian (Eds.), *Siting hazardous waste facilities: Local opposition and the myth of preemption*. Cambridge, MA: Ballinger Publishing, pp. 193–231.***

Onibokun, A. G., & Curry, M. (1976). An ideology of citizen participation: The Metropolitan Seattle Transit case study. *Public Administration Review, 36,* 269–277.*

Plumlee, J. P., Starling, J. D., with Kramer, K. W. (1985). Citizen participation in water quality planning: A case study of perceived failure. *Administration & Society, 16,* 445–473.*

Podolefsky, A. (1983). Community response to crime prevention: The Mission District. *Journal of Community Action, 1*, 43–48.*

Sklar, F., & Ames, R. G. (1985). Staying alive: Street tree survival in the inner-city. *Journal of Urban Affairs, 7*, 55–65.*

Stever, J. A. (1983). Citizen participation in negotiated investment strategy. *Journal of Urban Affairs, 5*, 231–240.*

Stewart, T. R., Dennis, R. L., & Ely, D .W. (1984). Citizen participation and judgment in policy analysis: A case study of urban air quality policy, *Policy Sciences, 17*, 67–87.*

Talbot, A. R. (1983). The Port Townsend Terminal. In A. R. Talbot (Ed.), *Settling things: Six case studies in environmental mediation.* Washington, DC: The Conservation Foundation and the Ford Foundation, pp. 78–89.**

References

Advisory Commission on Intergovernmental Relations. (1979). *In brief: Citizen participation in the American federal system*. Washington, DC: U.S. Government Printing Office.

Ahlbrandt, R. S., Jr., & Sumka, H. J. (1983). Neighborhood organizations and the coproduction of public services. *Journal of Urban Affairs, 5,* 211–220.

Arnstein, S. R. (1969). A ladder of citizen participation. *Journal of the American Institute of Planners, 35,* 216–224.

Bacot, H., Fitzgerald, M. R., Folz, D. H., McCabe, A. S., & Bowen, T. (1993). Practicing the politics of inclusion: Citizen surveys and the design of solid waste recycling programs. *American Review of Public Administration, 23,* 29–41.

Barber, B. R. (1984). *Strong democracy: Participatory politics for a new age*. Berkeley and Los Angeles: University of California Press.

Behn, R. D. (1991). *Leadership counts: Lessons for public managers*. Cambridge and London: Harvard University Press.

Bell, D., & Held, V. (1969). The community revolution. *The Public Interest, No. 42,* 142–177.

Berry, J. M., Portney, K. E., & Thomson, K. (1993). *The rebirth of urban democracy*. Washington, DC: The Brookings Institution.

Bingham, G. (1985). *Resolving environmental disputes: A decade of experience. Executive summary*. Washington, DC: The Conservation Foundation.

Brudney, J. L., & England, R. E. (1983). Toward a definition of the coproduction concept. *Public Administration Review, 43,* 59–65.

Brudney, J. L. (1990). *Fostering volunteer programs in the public sector*. San Francisco: Jossey-Bass.

Bryson, J. M., & Crosby, B. C. (1992). *Leadership for the common good: Tackling public problems in a shared-power world*. San Francisco: Jossey-Bass.

Carlson, C. (1983). Negotiated investment strategy: Mediating intergovernmental conflict. *National Forum: The Phi Kappa Phi Journal, 63,* 28–29.

Checkoway, B. (1981). The politics of public hearings. *Journal of Applied Behavioral Science, 17,* 566–582.

Chess, C., Long, S. K., & Sandman, P. M. (1990). *Making technical assistance grants work*. Camden, NJ: Rutgers University Press.

Cleveland, H. (1975). How do you get everybody in on the act and still get some action? *Public Management, 57, 3–6.*

Cleveland, H. (1985). The twilight of hierarchy: Speculations on the global information society. *Public Administration Review, 45, 185–195.*

Cogan, E. (1992). *Successful public meetings: A practical guide for managers in government.* San Francisco: Jossey-Bass.

Cohen, N. (1995). Technical assistance for citizen participation: A case study of New York City's environmental planning process. *American Review of Public Administration, 25, 119–135.*

Cole, R. L. (1974). *Citizen participation and the urban policy process.* Lexington, MA: Lexington Books.

Cole, R. L. (1981). Participation in community service organizations. *Journal of Community Action, 1, 53–60.*

Cole, R. L., and Caputo, D. A. (1984). The public hearing as an effective citizen participation mechanism. *American Political Science Review, 78,* 404–416.

Connor, D. M. (1988). A new ladder of citizen participation. *National Civic Review, 77, 249–257.*

Cooper, T. (1984). Citizenship and professionalism in public administration. *Public Administration Review, 44, 143–149.*

Cormick, G. W., & Patten, L. K. (1977). Environmental mediation: Defining the process through experience. Paper presented to the American Association for the Advancement of Science Symposium on Environmental Mediation Cases, Denver, Colorado.

Crosby, N., Kelly, J. M., & Schaefer, P. (1986). Citizens panels: A new approach to citizen participation. *Public Administration Review, 46, 170–178.*

Cupps, D. S. (1977). Emerging problems of citizen participation. *Public Administration Review, 37, 478–487.*

Desai, U. (1989). Public participation in environmental policy implementation: Case of the Surface Mining Control and Reclamation Act. *American Review of Public Administration, 19, 49–65.*

Dommel, P. R. (Ed.). (1982). *Decentralizing urban policy: Case studies in community development.* Washington, DC: The Brookings Institution.

Donald, D. (1994). Workshop offers option to express voters' views. *Savannah News-Press,* July 17, 6B.

Duncombe, S. (1985). Volunteers in city government: Advantages, disadvantages and uses. *National Civic Review, 74, 356–364.*

Dutton, D. (1984). The impact of public participation in biomedical policy: Evidence from four case studies. In J. C. Petersen (Ed.), *Citizen participation in science policy* (pp. 147–181). Amherst: University of Massachusetts Press.

Ebbin, S., & Kasper, R. (1974). *Citizen groups and the nuclear power controversy.* Cambridge, MA, and London: The MIT Press.

Fiedler, F. E. (1967). *A theory of leadership effectiveness.* New York: McGraw-Hill.

Field, R.H.G. (1979). A critique of the Vroom-Yetton contingency model of leadership behavior. *Academy of Management Review, 4,* 249–257.

Field, R.H.G. (1982). A test of the Vroom-Yetton normative model of leadership. *Journal of Applied Psychology, 67,* 523–532.

Fisher, R., & Brown, S. (1988). *Getting together: Building a relationship that gets to yes.* Boston: Houghton Mifflin.

Fisher, R., & Ury, W. (1983). *Getting to yes: Negotiating agreement without giving in.* New York: Penguin Books.

Fox, S. F. (1985). Who opposes public/private partnerships for urban renewal? A case study. *Journal of Urban Affairs, 7,* 27–40.

Freeman, R. E. (1984). *Strategic management: A stakeholder approach.* Marshfield, MA: Pitman Publishing.

Friedman, R. S. (1978). Representation in regulatory decision making: Scientific, industrial, and consumer inputs to the F.D.A. *Public Administration Review, 38,* 205–214.

Gillers, S. (1980). New faces in the neighborhood: Mediating the Forest Hills housing dispute. In R. B. Goldmann (Ed.), *Roundtable justice: Case studies in conflict resolution* (pp. 59–85). Boulder, CO: Westview Press.

Gittell, M., with Hoffacker, B., Rollins, E., Foster, S., & Hoffacker, M. (1980). *Limits to citizen participation: The decline of community organizations.* Beverly Hills, CA: Sage Publications.

Gittell, M. (1983). The consequences of mandating citizen participation. *Policy Studies Review, 3,* 90–95.

Goodnow, F. (1900). *Policy and administration.* New York: Macmillan.

Goodsell, C. T. (1983). *The case for bureaucracy: A public administration polemic.* Chatham, NJ: Chatham House Publishers.

Gormley, W. T., Jr. (1986). The representation revolution: Reforming state regulation through public representation. *Administration & Society, 18,* 179–196.

Gundry, K. G., & Heberlein, T. A. (1984). Do public meetings represent the public? *Journal of the American Planning Association, 50,* 175–182.

Haley, L. L. (1982). Community Development Block Grant implementation in Allegheny County, Pennsylvania. In P. R. Dommel (Ed.), *Decentralizing urban policy: Case studies in community development* (pp. 166–194). Washington, DC: The Brookings Institution.

Hallman, H. W. (1984). *Neighborhoods: Their place in urban life.* Beverly Hills: Sage Publications.

Harmon, M. M. (1971). Normative theory and public administration: Some suggestions for a redefinition of administrative responsibility. In F. Marini

(Ed.), *Toward a new public administration: The Minnowbrook perspective* (pp. 172–185). Scranton, PA: Chandler Publishing.

Harrington, M. (1962). *The other America: Poverty in the United States.* Baltimore, MD: Penguin Books.

Heberlein, T. A. (1976). Some observations on alternative mechanisms for public involvement: The hearing, public opinion poll, the workshop and the quasi-experiment. *Natural Resources Journal, 16,* 197–212.

Hendee, J. C., Lucas, R. C., Tracy, R. H., Staed, T., Clark, R. N., Stankey, G. H., & Yarnell, R. A. (1976). Methods for acquiring public input. In J. C. Pierce & H. R. Doerksen (Eds.), *Water politics and public involvement* (pp. 125–144). Ann Arbor, MI: Ann Arbor Science Publishers.

Huntington, S. P. (1975). The United States. In M. Crozier, S. P. Huntington & J. Watanuki (Eds.), *The crisis of democracy.* New York: New York University Press.

Jackson, J. S. (1982). Community Development Block Grant implementation in Carbondale, Illinois. In P. R. Dommel (Ed.), *Decentralizing urban policy: Case studies in community development* (pp. 195–222). Washington, DC: The Brookings Institution.

John, D. (1994). Civic environmentalism. *Issues in Science and Technology, 10,* 30–34.

Johnson, K. F., & Hein, C. J. (1983). Municipal use of citizen surveys. *Journal of Urban Affairs, 5,* 241–248.

Judd, D. R. (1979). *The politics of American cities: Private power and public policy.* Boston: Little, Brown.

Kemmis, D. (1990). *Community and the politics of place.* Norman, OK: University of Oklahoma Press.

The Kettering Foundation. (1991). *Citizens and politics: A view from Main Street America.* Dayton, OH: The Kettering Foundation.

Kettl, D. F. (1981). The fourth face of federalism. *Public Administration Review, 41,* 366–371.

Kihl, M. R. (1985). The viability of public hearings in transportation planning. *Journal of Applied Behavioral Science, 21,* 185–200.

Kirlin, J. J. (1973). The impact of increasing lower-status clientele upon city governmental structures: A model from organization theory. *Urban Affairs Quarterly, 8,* 317–343.

Krislov, S. (1974). *Representative bureaucracy.* Englewood Cliffs, NJ: Prentice-Hall.

Lan, Z., & Rosenbloom, D. H. (1992). Public administration in transition? *Public Administration Review, 52,* 535–537.

LaPorte, T. R. (1971). The recovery of relevance in the study of public organizations. In F. Marini (Ed.), *Toward a new public administration: The Minnowbrook perspective* (pp. 17–48). Scranton, PA: Chandler Publishing.

Levin, M. A., & Sanger, M. B. (1994). *Making government work: How entrepreneurial executives turn bright ideas into results*. San Francisco: Jossey-Bass.

Levine, C. (1984). Citizenship and service delivery: The promise of coproduction. *Public Administration Review, 44*, 178–187.

Lineberry, R. L. (1983). *Government in America: People, politics, and policy* (2nd ed). Boston: Little, Brown.

Lipsky, M. (1968). Protest as a political resource. *American Political Science Review, 62*, 1144–1158.

Lipsky, M. (1971). Street-level bureaucracy and the analysis of urban reform. *Urban Affairs Quarterly, 6*, 391–409.

Lobel, I. B. (1992). The Killington/Pico mediation project. *Resolve: A Newsletter on Environmental Dispute Resolution, No. 25*, 6–8.

MacNair, R. H., Caldwell, R., & Pollane, L. (1983). Citizen participants in public bureaucracies: Foul-weather friends. *Administration & Society, 14*, 507–524.

Manring, N. J. (1993). Reconciling science and politics in Forest Service decision making: New tools for public administrators. *American Review of Public Administration, 23*, 343–359.

McCarthy, H. B., & Howitt, A. M. (1984). Extending the Red Line to Arlington. In A. M. Howitt (Ed.), *Managing federalism* (pp. 270–295). Washington, DC: Congressional Quarterly Press.

McClendon, B. W., & Lewis, J. A. (1985). Goals for Corpus Christi: Citizen participation in planning. *National Civic Review, 74*, 72–80.

McGuire, M., Rubin, B., Agranoff, R., & Richards, C. (1994). Building development capacity in nonmetropolitan communities. *Public Administration Review, 54*, 426–433.

Milbrath, L. W. (1981). Citizen surveys as citizen participation mechanisms. *Journal of Applied Behavioral Science, 17*, 478–496.

Miller, T. I., & Miller, M. A. (1991). *Citizen surveys: How to do them, how to use them, what they mean*. Washington, DC: International City Management Association.

Murray, M. A. (1983). Comparing public and private management: An exploratory essay. In J. L. Perry & K. L. Kraemer (Eds.), *Public management: Public and private perspectives* (pp. 60–71). Palo Alto, CA: Mayfield Publishing.

Needleman, M. L., & Needleman, C. E. (1974). *Guerrillas in the bureaucracy: The community planning experiment in the United States*. New York: Wiley.

Nelkin, D. (1984). Science and technology policy and the democratic process. In James C. Petersen (Ed.), *Citizen participation in science policy* (pp. 18–39). Amherst, MA: University of Massachusetts Press.

Osborne, D., Gaebler, T. (1993). *Reinventing government: How the entrepreneurial spirit is transforming the public sector*. Reading, MA: Penguin Books.

Percy, S. L. (1987). Citizen involvement in coproducing safety and security in the community. *Public Productivity Review, 42*, 83–93.

Peters, T. J., & Waterman, R. H., Jr. (1982). *In search of excellence*. New York: Harper & Row.

Petersen, J. C. (Ed.). (1984). *Citizen participation in science policy*. Amherst, MA: University of Massachusetts Press.

Peterson, P. E. (1970). Forms of representation: Participation of the poor in the Community Action Program. *American Political Science Review, 64*, 491–507.

Plumlee, J. P., & Starling, J. D., with Kramer, K. W. (1985). Citizen participation in water quality planning: A case study of perceived failure. *Administration & Society, 16*, 455–473.

Polilli, S. (1994). Dial G for government: Logging on to your friendly city hall. *Governing: The Magazine of States and Localities, 7*, January, 25–26.

Pressman, J. L. (1975). *Federal programs and city politics: The dynamics of the aid process in Oakland*. Berkeley and Los Angeles: University of California Press.

Riedel, J. A. (1972). Citizen participation: Myths and realities. *Public Administration Review, 32*, 211–220.

Rodgers, R., & Hunter, J. E. (1992). A foundation of good management practice in government: Management by Objectives. *Public Administration Review, 52*, 27–39.

Rourke, F. E. (1992). Responsiveness and neutral competence in American bureaucracy. *Public Administration Review, 52*, 539–546.

Rydell, R. J. (1984). Solving political problems of nuclear technology: The role of public participation. In J. C. Petersen (Ed.), *Citizen participation in science policy* (pp. 182–195). Amherst, MA: University of Massachusetts Press.

Scavio, C. (1993). The use of participative mechanisms by large U.S. cities. *Journal of Urban Affairs, 15*, 93–109.

Schwarz, R. M. (1994). *The skilled facilitator: Practical wisdom for developing effective groups*. San Francisco: Jossey-Bass.

Sembor, E. (1992). Building community citizenship through study circles. *Public Management*, June, 15–17.

Sharp, E. B. (1986). *Citizen demand-making in the urban context*. University, AL: The University of Alabama Press.

Sharp, E. B. (1990). *Urban politics and administration: From service delivery to economic development*. New York and London: Longman.

Sklar, F., & Ames, R. G. (1985). Staying alive: Street tree survival in the inner-city. *Journal of Urban Affairs, 7*, 55–65.

Stipak, B. (1983). Toward more thoughtful and responsible use of public opinion data by local administrators. *Journal of Urban Affairs, 5*, 249–256.

Stivers, C. (1994). The listening bureaucrat: Responsiveness in public administration. *Public Administration Review, 54*, 364–369.

Sullivan, T. J. (1984). *Resolving development disputes through negotiations*. New York and London: Plenum Press.

Talbot, A. R. (1983). *Settling things: Six case studies in environmental mediation*. Washington, DC: The Conservation Foundation and the Ford Foundation.

Thomas, J. C. (1982). Citizen-initiated contacts with government agencies: A test of three theories. *American Journal of Political Science, 26*, 504–522.

Thomas, J. C. (1986). *Between citizen and city: Neighborhood organizations and urban politics in Cincinnati*. Lawrence: University Press of Kansas.

Thomas, J. C. (1987). Neighborhood coproduction and municipal productivity. *Public Productivity Review, 42*, 83–93.

Thomas, J. C. (1990). Public involvement in public management: Adapting and testing a borrowed theory. *Public Administration Review, 50*, 435–445.

Thomas, J. C. (1993). Public involvement and governmental effectiveness: A decision-making model for public managers. *Administration & Society, 24*, 444–469.

Tipple, T. J., & Wellman, J. D. (1991). Herbert Kaufman's Forest Ranger thirty years later: From simplicity and homogeneity to complexity and diversity. *Public Administration Review, 51*, 421–428.

Using public rage for private ends. (1993). *Kansas City Star*, March 17, pp. A1, A12.

Van Meter, E. C. (1975). Citizen participation in the policy management process. *Public Administration Review, 35*, 804–812.

Vedlitz, A., & Veblen, E. P. (1980). Voting and contacting: Two forms of political participation in a suburban community. *Urban Affairs Quarterly, 16*, 31–48.

Verba, S., & Nie, N. H. (1972). *Participation in America*. New York: Harper & Row.

Vogel, R. K., & Swanson, B. E. (1988). Setting agendas for community change: The community goal-setting strategy. *Journal of Urban Affairs, 10*, 41–61.

Vroom, V. H. (1976). Can leaders learn to lead? *Organizational Dynamics, 4*, 17–28.

Vroom, V. H., & Jago, A. G. (1978). On the validity of the Vroom-Yetton model. *Journal of Applied Psychology, 63*, 151–162.

Vroom, V. H., & Jago, A. G. (1988). *The new leadership: Managing participation in organizations*. Englewood Cliffs, NJ: Prentice-Hall.

Vroom, V. H., & Yetton, P. (1973). *Leadership and decision making*. Pittsburgh: University of Pittsburgh Press.

Walker, J. L. (1983). The origins and maintenance of interest groups in America. *American Political Science Review, 77*, 390–406.

Watson, D. J., Juster, R. J., & Johnson, G. W. (1991). Institutionalized use of citizen surveys in the budgetary and policy-making processes: A small city case study. *Public Administration Review, 51,* 232–239.

Webb, K., & Hatry, H. P. (1973). *Obtaining citizen feedback: The application of citizen surveys to local governments.* Washington, DC: The Urban Institute.

Webber, M. M. (1974). Alternative styles for citizen participation in transport planning. *Transportation Research Record, 356,* 6–11.

Wheeland, C. M. (1993). Citywide strategic planning: An evaluation of Rock Hill's Empowering the Vision. *Public Administration Review, 53,* 65–72.

Whitaker, G. P. (1980). Coproduction: Citizen participation in service delivery. *Public Administration Review, 40,* 240–246.

Whorton, J. W., & Worthley, J. A. (1983). A perspective on the challenge of public management: Environmental paradox and organizational culture. In J. L. Perry and K. L. Kraemer (Eds.). *Public management: Public and private perspectives* (pp. 126–132). Palo Alto, CA: Mayfield Publishing.

Wilson, W. (1887). The study of administration. *Political Science Quarterly, 2,* 197–232.

Yates, D. (1977). *The ungovernable city: The politics of urban problems and policy making.* Cambridge, MA: The MIT Press.

Yin, R., & Yates, D. (1974). Street-level governments: Assessing decentralization and urban services. *Nation's Cities,* November, 34–48.

Index

A

Action centers, 154–156
Advisory Commission on Intergovernmental Relations, 4
Advisory committees, 12, 82–83, 86–88, 120–126, 149, 150; advantages and disadvantages of, 121–123; membership selection in, 122–123; in regulatory decision making, 4, 124–126; and relevant public, 51, 123–124; and sharing of influence. *See also* Citizen groups
Agranoff, R., 166
Ahlbrandt, R. S., Jr., 33, 160
Ames, R. G., 77
Arnstein, S. R., 41
Atomic Energy Commission (AEC), 53–54
Auburn, Alabama, resident surveys in, 105

B

Bacot, H., 106–107
Barber, B. R., 6, 109, 141
Behn, R. D., 170
Bell, D., 165
Bellingham, Washington, economic development initiative, 81–83, 86–87
Berry, J. M., 138, 143, 150, 164, 165
Bingham, G., 127, 129, 130
Bowen, T., 106–107
Brown, S., 139, 140, 141, 157, 174
Brudney, J. L., 156, 161, 162, 163
Bryson, J. M., 177, 179

C

Caldwell, R., 29
Caputo, D. A., 5
Checkoway, B., 33, 114, 115, 119
Chess, C., 149
Cincinnati, Ohio: community councils in, 8–10, 65–67, 143–145; coproduction in, 159; school tax levy campaign in, 166–167
Citizen contacts, 13
Citizen panels, 116
Citizen surveys, 12–13, 40, 63, 87, 102–108
Citizen groups: allocation powers of, 150–151; favorable climate for, 176; funding for, 148–149; government assistance for, 147–151; and mediation, 128–129; in municipal governments, 157–158, 159, 163–164; and the public interest, 164–167; representativeness assessment of, 64–68; technical assistance for, 149–150. *See also* Advisory committees; Neighborhood groups
Citizen-manager relationship, 137–151; citizen education in, 142–145; communication in, 140; leadership commitment in, 138–139; learning process in, 143–146; managers' reliability in, 141; and need for informed public, 141–147; process issues versus outcome issues in, 139; risk averse strategy in, 140
Civil service personnel systems, 18
Clark, R. N., 94, 95, 117
Cleveland, H., 5, 6, 28, 33, 37, 178, 187

205